MW01171143

i

THE UNIQUELY CHRISTIAN WORLDVIEW

PAUL ETHINGTON

The Uniquely Christian Worldview © 2019 by Paul M. Ethington.

All rights reserved. No part of this book may be reproduced in any form or by any electronic or mechanical means including information storage and retrieval systems, without permission in writing from the author. The only exception is by a reviewer, who may quote short excerpts in a review.

Author: Paul M. Ethington

Unless otherwise indicated, all Scripture quotations are from The Holy Bible, The New King James Version, Copyright © 1982 by Thomas Nelson, Inc.

Printed in the United States of America

First printing Dec 2019

SDBN 9781674904702

This book is dedicated to Prof. Samir Massouh, Trinity International Univ, Deerfield, IL, who came here from Lebanon in the 60's and was a fellow student and friend in the Philosophy Dept. at Cal State Univ, Fullerton. Samir's wonderful intellect spurred me to get below the surface of things and to think deeply. His Sincere Christian faith, love for classical music and pursuit of truth was always a beautifully motivating thing for me.

CONTENTS

PREFACE

This project began with my participation in a Christian philosophy group called Mars Hill in Newport Beach, California. The group was founded by the late Bob and Gretchen Passantino and was moderated by Ken Sands at the time. Earlier I had earned a bachelor in philosophy before going on to a music degree, but I minored in English and history. That might explain why I would take on a task involving the philosophy of history. For this endeavor I had to dig into my courses on western civilization, philosophy and literary theory. Additionally, I just had to do a lot of reading. Cited in this book are more than 130 authors and persons. The more I wrestled with the subject the more the idea of the book became clear.

Christianity is a historical religion (if it is a religion at all); Christian apologetics must necessarily include historical apologetics in my view because at every turn it must reflect what God has done, not just what He said. It is the story of the birth, life, death and resurrection of Jesus. That true story is bolstered by a foundational mountain of verifiable history which gives us full confidence in God's Word and, most of all, in the purposes of God in creation and redemption. It tells of His calling a people for Himself in Israel that He might bless the whole world through them. It tells of His intention to build His church, and it tells how the story will end. His plan unfolds in the progressive revelation of thousands of years of history. So if one is to have a proper Christian worldview, it must be built on that history, not only on modern Western civilization or on the current trends of our short lives.

With a broad understanding of the origins of our faith together with grounding in essential doctrine we can approach the treacherous task of studying world religions, secular points of view and rifts within Christianity over doctrinal nuance. We can get a better view of why Christianity is so amazingly universal and not merely culture bound. One thing is certain, not only is the statement that "a little bit of truth can be found in each religion" inane, but these belief systems are totally dissimilar from Christianity where truth is claimed with a capital "T." Its worldview is simply not the same as other worldviews. To be a little bit Christian is not to be a Christian at all.

I have tried to place other worldviews in the context of metaphor to show how they are so different than biblical Christianity. I have also put together a primer on the main religions of the world to show that they have nothing in common with Christianity. Finally, I hope that I have shown secular humanism to be another false religion through which the deception of Satan has blinded the world to God's revelation. We can learn from history. Either it will cause us to lose hope that mankind will ever change for the better, or it will reveal that God has done all that He should to communicate His love for mankind, His warnings for all of us who would run headlong into self-destruction and His amazing provision for our eternal salvation.

At the suggestion of Gretchen Passantino, I have placed in the appendix a glossary for quick reference so that the vocabulary used in this book can be accessible to everyone. There are plenty of "technical" words in here which are used not to impress but to make clear, for it is better to be clear than clever. It is hoped that the presentation's generalizations, particularly with regard to a Christian's Worldview, are easily seen and understood.

PART I
THE BIG PICTURE

CHAPTER 1
THE IMPORTANCE OF A CHRISTIAN WORLDVIEW

The World is Getting Smaller

Ravi Zacharias brings us this insight: At a time in our cultural history when the West is looking more like the East and the East is covertly trying to emulate the West, understanding the exceptionality of Christianity is all the more needed. Religions are making a revival, but often as a hybrid of western marketing techniques and eastern mythology – a devastating combination of seduction through media and mysticism. The first casualty in such a mix is truth, and, consequently, the person of God.[1] Much is being made of a modern movement in Christianity called "the emergent church." With these church leaders evangelism is human persuasion. They boast in large congregations and innovative outreach to the un-churched. They endeavor to be non-threatening to the seeker and to create an atmosphere of familiarity and comfort. The severe warnings of the Scriptures are carefully avoided and only the "good news" is preached (God's love without God's holiness). As they borrow from Eastern religions and *"proof-text"* their happy gospel, avoiding careful *exegesis* [2] of the Scriptures, they often present a non-biblical world view and a distorted Christianity. So how can we avoid a merely cultural *worldview*?

Developing a Worldview

When I see the world around me, even my own life, I see it through a set of *presuppositions*. Learning began with my own biological senses, discovering my limitations, deciding what worked, what was safe and what brought reward. It progressed with thought processes which categorized, predicted and compared. I was willing to place facts and ideas in abeyance for verification and refinement. But I was not able to assemble a complete framework, a complete belief system, which took all things into account. It took great leaps as I chose to trust the testimony of others and to reach beyond my immediate experience. James W. Sire sees this process as the subjective desire to satisfy the need for truth, and that it may be lack of truth that causes us to investigate our world view in the first place. The vague uneasy feeling that we have that something doesn't fit causes us to seek satisfaction. Our worldview is not quite livable. We bury our doubt, but it rises to the surface. We mask our insecurity, but our mask falls off. We find, in fact, that it is only when we pursue our doubts and search for the truth that we begin to get real satisfaction.[3]

For my worldview I would develop *presuppositions* on the authority of God's Word and of those whom I could trust within that authority. These tenants are foundational to my belief system and require no further proof. The world is too large and I am too limited to feign omniscience. "Worldview" not only involves these decisions and influences but the existence of a consistent and identifiable set of parameters, a resident structure within the mind and heart which makes one's choices and perceptions consistent and dependable. Arbitrary choices and capricious behaviors are disallowed. Unreasonable behaviors are scrutinized as lacking integrity. Behaviors merely derived from the socially acceptable and politically correct are called into question. When ones worldview produces what appears to some as outlandish, others may ask, "Where on earth did you get that idea?" If I am a Christian, the answer had better be an honest examination of that derived from Christ. Do I really have a "Christian" worldview?

> These [Bereans] were more fair-minded than those in Thessalonica, in that they received the word with all readiness, and searched the Scriptures daily to find out whether these things were so (Acts 17:11).

Let's just start at the beginning. Think of the Genesis account. God created Adam and Eve in His own image. He invited Adam to join in creation by naming the animals. His first reflection about Adam was that he needed a companion. You might say God's first interaction with human beings was a teaching session: He told them to reproduce themselves and to fill the earth. He told them to care for His creation. He told them to work the ground and use its bounties for food. Not least, in telling them not to eat of a certain tree, He was telling them to restrain their impulses and be obedient to his authority. So God created people with needs. He gave them hunger so they would eat and survive. He gave them sexual urges that would encourage human intimacy and ensure mating and procreation. Would He then leave them without a spiritual appetite to prompt them toward their ultimate reason for being? No. He created them with a God-need, to which His Spirit would speak, drawing them to Himself. Powerful needs for love and belonging move people to form caring relationships with Him and other humans.

Because humankind's basic purpose is to be with God, our primary need is to be in harmony with Him. This need leads to searching and learning, and so we develop *the image of God* qualities. Our need to think and choose, to create, and to become all we were meant to be makes us potentially more godly or Christ-like. The Bible begins with God creating humans and giving them instructions concerning His purpose for people and nature. From the Genesis creation account to the Great Commission recorded in Matthew's Gospel, the Bible is a story of how God works through people to generate and maintain His purpose. Our purpose is God's purpose. Sin entered our nature when this potential to be like God was misused. The fall of Adam and Eve is the original demonstration of how all evils and troubles come from not understanding real human needs or from trying to meet them in wrong ways.[4]

Becoming Our Own God

I will never forget the surprise on the face of my friend when he discovered through a small-group experience that he was prejudiced against the black race. "How could this have happened to me?" he asked. "Selective sampling," I replied. He understood what I was getting at. We human beings see what we want to see and overlook that which we do not. We have a strong desire to categorize, exclude and simplify. Some of this is over-efficiency in managing the computer of the mind; some of it is laziness; but a large part of this "selective sampling" is rooted in sin, i.e. rejection of biblical teaching, rebellion against God's boundaries, disobedience of God's direction or perversion of God's design.

> *There is neither Jew nor Greek, there is neither slave nor free, there is neither male nor female; for you are all one in Christ Jesus* (Gal 3:28).

We just want to believe what we want to believe and do what we want to do. We try to become our own gods. Ironically, we may be stepping into Satan's devouring jaws, hardly in control of our own destiny. I have noted that the Charles Mansons of this world are bent on creating their own reality, their own truth and their own guidelines.

In those days there was no king in Israel; everyone did what was right in his own eyes (Judges 21:25).

Testing Our Own Presuppositions

Perhaps this problem is more widespread than Charles Manson. It is clear that we need a way of looking at ourselves, at life and at God which invites the truth and avoids self-deception. No man is without *presuppositions*, but he can be free from deceit. He can at least apply certain tests to his worldview. He can ask, "Is my *worldview* internally consistent and reasonable? Does it match up with my experience and that of others? Is the scheme pragmatic (does it work)?" How honest am I being in the adoption of my *worldview*? What are my presuppositions; on what do I base my *worldview*?"

My own presuppositions are that God exists and that he has my best interest in mind (Heb 11:6). When He beckoned me, I chose to trust Him. I have been rewarded with great peace of mind, as well as blessings undeserved or earned. I am a child of his loving kindness. Christ paid the price for my sins by His crucifixion and atonement. He brings hope through His resurrection and purpose through His example and teaching. He is a personal Christ who walks and talks with me by His Spirit (Heb 13:5). It took no secret knowledge for this personal discovery, because through the gospel the "sound has gone out (Rom 10:18)" and "He was not willing that any should perish (2 Pet 3:9)." Jesus included me when I "believed on Him through their word" (John 17:20). I am persuaded that the Christian Bible is truly God's Word in man's language, that it is surely the inspired testament of our Creator.

But how can I claim that I arrived at these beliefs other than by *"selective sampling?"* How can I know that I have found the truth? Of course, these are questions of *epistemology*, but more importantly, of *worldview*. How do I look at the world? What are my presuppositions (not presumptions)? What motivates me? What brings purpose to everything? A monotheistic *worldview* causes me to relinquish my propensity for control, my self-centeredness; and to place God squarely in the center of the design. That would seem to include Judaism, Islam and Christianity. It may even include the "higher power" of twelve-step programs. What then distinguishes the Christian *worldview* from others?

John Byl's Explanation of Christian Worldview

John Byl's book, *The Divine Challenge*, answers the question in terms of the struggle between God and man over who will rule. In this context Byl shows the superiority of the Christian *worldview* over its main competitors. Only Christianity is coherent and meaningful. The challenges of modern *naturalism* and *post-modern relativism* ultimately self-destruct. Using Roger Penrose's concept of "three worlds and three mysteries" found in matter, mind and math, Shadows of the Mind, 1994, Byl asks why mathematical laws play such a large role in the physical universe, how the physical world of matter can produce perceiving minds and how a perceiving mind can create mathematical concepts.

These are great mysteries that deserve an answer not found in any other *worldview* than Christianity. The others leave us with no firm foundation for either truth or morals. What are the *presuppositions* of the Christian *worldview*? [5]

1. God is the Ultimate Reality

    A. God is sovereign
    B. God is All-Powerful
    C. God Knows Everything
    D. God is a Spirit
    E. God is Tri-Personal
    F. God is Everywhere
    G. God is Good
    H. God is Infinite

2. The Universe Totally Depends on God

    A. All Things Were Created by God
    B. God Created Freely
    C. The World Always Depends on God
    D. Creation out of Nothing

3. Man Was Created to Be God's Steward

    A. Created in the Image of God
    B. The Fall and Its Fall-Out
    C. Redemption Through Christ

4. God Created Man to Know

    A. The Bible is Our Standard
    B. Our Faculties Were Created to be Reliable
    C. Our Heart is in Control

5. God Sets the Standards

6. History Unfolds God's Plan

One of the most helpful testimonies of how one acquires a Christian *worldview* comes from Edgar R. Lee. He writes, "Without my being consciously aware of technical issues, the Bible began to fill in my understanding of the origin of humankind, the meaning and purpose of our life on earth, and the nature of our eternal destiny. So early on I learned that God is Creator of everything, human beings have fallen into sin and are in desperate need of redemption, Jesus Christ died and rose again for our sins, and He is coming again to finally reconcile the universe to Himself. When the evangelist called for my "decision," I already knew the basic elements of a Christian *worldview*."[6]

Since the Christian *worldview* flows from the Bible, the key Christian presupposition is that the Bible is God's written Word and, as such, the absolute standard of truth. The prime *worldview* teaching of the Bible is the total sovereignty of God, who is the ultimate reality. Furthermore, the Christian worldview survives these general criteria for any viable worldview:

1. Is this *worldview* internally coherent?
2. Is this *worldview* consistent with experience?
3. Is this *worldview* livable?

To these the Christian adds:

4. Does this *worldview* stand the test of Scripture?
5. Does this *worldview* present sufficient reason to believe it, i.e. does everything that happens have a place in God's purposeful, all-encompassing plan? Consequently, does it uphold the principle of causality, i.e. everything that happens is caused, directly or indirectly, by God?

Byl warns against the danger of compromise. *Worldviews come as package deals.* Compromising Christianity with modern, post-modern or pagan ideals introduces an inconsistency into our lives that will eventually undermine our commitment to God. 'No man can serve two masters' (Matt 6:24). Likewise, no inconsistent worldview can hope to survive. Hence, we should diligently test the spirits of the day, discerning their source and implications.[7]

> *And be not conformed to this world: but be ye*
> *transformed by the renewing of your mind, that ye*
> *may prove what is that good, and acceptable, and*
> *perfect, will of God* (Rom 12:2)

This is no easy thing. It is difficult to avoid contamination from the society in which we live. It requires us to test and cleanse our every thought, bringing it in line with God's Word and will:

> *For the weapons of our warfare are not carnal, but*
> *mighty through God to the pulling down of*
> *strongholds; casting down imaginations, and every*
> *high thing that exalteth itself against the knowledge of*
> *God, and bringing into captivity every thought to the*
> *obedience of Christ* (2 Cor 10:4-5).

> *For we wrestle not against flesh and blood, but against*
> *principalities, against powers, against the rulers of the*
> *darkness of this world, against spiritual wickedness in*
> *high places* (Eph 6:12).

Christianity, like its rivals, is all-embracing. Hence, worldview wars are total wars, covering every aspect of reality. The Christian must therefore be constantly alert, relying on God and applying the full armor he supplies:

> *Finally, my brethren, be strong in the Lord, and in the power of his might. Put on the whole armor of God, that ye may be able to stand against the wiles of the devil* (Eph 6:10-11).

In his concluding Chapter 15, "The Challenge Settled," John Byl summarized the nature of *worldviews:*

We stressed that the question was one of opposing *worldviews.* Everyone has a *worldview,* although most people may be unaware that they are viewing reality through the spectacles that a particular *worldview* provides. All worldviews are based on *presuppositions,* on basic initial assumptions about reality that are rarely stated explicitly. Such worldview presuppositions set our standards for what we consider to be reasonable. Different worldviews may entail radically different views of rationality. Nevertheless, conflicting *worldviews* can usually be assessed in terms of quite general criteria such as consistency, experience and livability. Any viable worldview must be able to accommodate the basic commonsense notions needed for normal conversation and scientific activity. In particular, we stressed the necessity of truth and logic, as well as the importance of the principle of sufficient reason. Embracing a *worldview* is not a dry academic exercise. Our *worldview* sets the direction for our life. It determines the path we follow and the goals we seek. It guides us in deciding how to live our lives. Our answers to *worldview* questions are matters of life and death.[8]

Trust and Intellectual Humility

If John Byl is right, we cannot adopt a candy-store mentality whereby we decide to accept this and that from the Scripture without accepting the rest. We may argue over the interpretation of a particular passage or the preeminence of a certain doctrine. We may "see through a glass darkly" as in Paul's explanation of our current state of "corruption," but we are aware in our faith-step that there is an underpinning of full *revelation*:

> *Now I only know in part, but then I shall know just as I also am known* (1 Cor 13:12)

We are not God, but we reflect the image of God. He reveals Himself to us by general, progressive and direct *revelation*. That we can understand Him can be explained only in terms of His preparation of our minds and hearts to understand. "Show me Your glory," said Moses to God. God replied, "I will put you in the cleft of the rock, and will cover you with My hand while I pass by. Then I will take away My hand, and you shall see My back; but My face shall not be seen (Exod 33:18-23)." And that will be sufficient (by implication). And then in that wonderful balance found throughout scripture, He says through the prophet Isaiah,

> *Seek the Lord while He may be found, call upon Him while He is near. Let the wicked forsake his way, and the unrighteous man his thoughts. Let him return to the Lord, and He will have mercy on him; and to our God, for He will abundantly pardon. For My thoughts are not your thoughts, nor are your ways My ways, says the Lord* (Isaiah 55:6-8).

"Oh, that I knew where I might find Him," we cry out! Though infinite, God has not made Himself inaccessible. We are encouraged to understand by acknowledging Him:

> *Trust in the Lord with all your heart, and lean not on your own understanding; in all your ways acknowledge Him, and He shall direct your paths (Prov 3:5-6).*

> *For I know the thoughts that I think toward you, says the Lord, thoughts of peace and not of evil, to give you a future and a hope. Then you will call upon Me and go and pray to Me, and I will listen to You. And you will seek Me and find Me, when you search for Me with all your heart (Jer 29:11-13).*

Man versus God

Without such a *worldview* we would easily be discouraged, confused and misguided by influences other than God. Without it we might try to lay human autonomy as the foundation of our worldview, reminiscent of the Tower of Babel in Genesis 11. Its first floor might be science, which gives understanding, its second floor technology, which gives it power, and its third floor economics, which gives purpose for the rest. The fourth floor may be consumerism, feeding superficial pleasures and driving the economy.[9]

Sound familiar? That we live in a Christian society may be more a sentimental statement than one of particular honesty. Is Byl's Babel *metaphor* consistent with Christianity? Often, in fact, our culture wars against the Christian worldview. In America we are pragmatic but lack purpose and direction. No longer do we have "unum" in our "pluribus." We do not even have unity within our churches. In this humanistic environment, in this celebration of diversity and distrust of authority, do we facilitate our defense of the faith and our evangelistic fervor with a consistent Christian worldview? Because, without it we are not salt; we are not light.

If we don't really believe the truth of God and live it, then our witness will be confusing and misleading. Most of us go through life not recognizing that our personal worldviews have been deeply affected by the world. Through the media and other influences, the secularized American view of history, law, politics, science, God and man affects our thinking more than we realize. We then are taken "captive through hollow and deceptive philosophy, which depends on human tradition and the basic principles of this world rather than on Christ" (Colossians 2:8). However, by diligently learning, applying and trusting God's truths in every area of our lives, whether it's watching a movie, communicating with our spouses, raising our children or working at the office, we can begin to develop a deep comprehensive faith that will stand against the unrelenting tide of our culture's non-biblical ideas. If we capture and embrace more of God's worldview and trust it with unwavering faith, then we begin to make the right decisions and form the appropriate responses to questions on abortion, same- sex marriage, cloning, stem-cell research and even media choices, because, in the end, it is our decisions and actions that reveal what we really believe.[10]

Do not conform any longer to the pattern of this world, but be transformed by the renewing of your mind (Rom 12:2).

Ultimate Purpose

R.C. Sproul in his book, <u>The Consequences of Ideas</u>, relates this story:

My personal baptism into the public education crisis occurred in the 1960s when we sent our firstborn, our daughter, off to first grade.... After a few weeks the school hosted a parents' night in which the principal would explain the school's philosophy of education. I attended eagerly. The principal... was both winsome and articulate.... He went through each segment of the school day, demonstrating that every moment was spent in purposeful activity. This tour de force overwhelmed the audience with its detailed and erudite explanation of every element in the curriculum. When finished he asked, "Are there any questions?" Spontaneous laughter erupted. Only a fool would raise a question after the principal had so masterfully covered all the bases. I risked everyone's disdain by raising my hand.... I said: "Sir, I am profoundly impressed by your careful analysis. You have made it clear that you do everything for a purpose. But there are only so many minutes in a day, and therefore you must be selective in choosing what specific purposes you want to achieve. My question is, Why did you select the particular purposes you have chosen? What is the ultimate purpose you use to decide which particular purposes you select? In other words, what kind of child are you trying to produce and why?" The principal's face turned ashen, then beet-red. Without rancor and with humility, he replied: "I don't know. Nobody has ever asked me that question." "Sir," I responded, "I deeply appreciate your candor and your spirit, but frankly, your answer terrifies me." What I heard in this public forum was pragmatism with a vengeance. There were purposes without purpose, truths without truth. There was no norm to determine what is ultimately pragmatic. Jesus' words, "What profit is it to a man if he gains the whole world, and loses his own soul (Matt 16:26)?"

According to Sproul we have been suffocated by *naturalism*, but have refused to open the door to a transcendent God. He quotes Etienne Gilson (1884-1978) who defined modern philosophy as "*mere by-products born of* the philosophical decomposition of the Christian living God." James Sire tells us that nihilism is the natural child of naturalism.[11] Sproul continued:

Jesus was being practical. He was saying that every practical goal of proximate success sooner or later must be measured against an ultimate norm for its ultimate practical result.[12]

Gilson insisted that our real choice in philosophy is between the *skepticism* of Emmanuel Kant and the theism of Thomas Aquinas. Sproul contends that we need to reconstruct the classical synthesis by which *natural theology* bridges the *special revelation* of Scripture and the *general revelation* of nature. The thinking person could embrace nature without embracing naturalism. All of life, in its unity and diversity, could be lived *coram Deo*, before the face of God, under His authority and to His glory.[13]

If we are to represent our Savior to our contemporaries, we need to adopt His *worldview*, that is, the "Christian *worldview*." We do not have to compromise for political correctness or fear of offense.

For the message of the cross is foolishness to those who are perishing, but to us who are being saved it is the power of God (1 Cor 1:18).

To that end we turn to the basic question and litmus test of the Christian: "Is my *worldview* biblical?"

CHAPTER 2
THINKING BIBLICALLY

In order to have a Christian worldview the believer presupposes the Truth of God, that there is a source made available to man for truth with a capital "T." "What is truth?" asked Pilot of Jesus. Jesus had already prayed for us in the Garden of Gethsemane, "Sanctify them in Your truth, Your Word is truth" (John 17:17). The Christian is separated from the error of the unbeliever and made whole through God's intervention. This intervention is "the Way, the Truth and the Life" offered by Jesus Christ (John 14:1-7). "The Word became flesh and dwelt among us" (John 1:14). The only thing that is completely reliable as truth is the word of God. This view is rooted in the Scripture's testimony about itself and the fact that the Bible is inerrant.

All Scripture is given by inspiration of God, and is profitable for doctrine, for reproof, for correction, for instruction in righteousness, that the man of god may be complete, thoroughly equipped for every good work (2 Tim 3:16-17).

For prophecy never came by the will of man, but holy men of God spoke as they were moved by the Holy Spirit (2 Pet 1:21).

In hope of eternal life which God, who cannot lie, promised before time began, but has in due time manifested His word through preaching, which was committed to me according to the commandment of God our Savior (Titus 1:1-3).

For I am the Lord, I do not change; therefore you are not consumed, O sons of Jacob (Malachi 3:6).

God's Word reflects the character of God; He does not change and His Word does not change. Arthur F. Holmes affirmed that "all truth is God's truth."[14] Holmes objected to the bifurcation of truth between spiritual and natural, between faith and science. The result of such dualistic perspective is that the overall authority and reliability of the Bible is undermined, because some areas of Scripture are not allowed to be brought to bear on scholarship. One cannot separate a sacred from a secular point of Scripture, because God cannot be separated from his creation. A worldview that would claim to be biblical must be one that can be harmonized with Scripture at every point of intersection. The worldview of most individuals has its value determined by a variety of means, with science playing a major role. Sometimes the issue is utilitarian, whether the worldview works in the sense that it explains reality. But the search for the correct worldview apart from biblical Christianity can never lead to the one reliable methodology that comprehensively intersects Truth and reality. It is at this juncture that the immovable Word of God resides.[15]

What essentially distinguishes the Christian worldview from other worldviews? At the heart of the matter, a Christian worldview contrasts with competing worldviews in that it:

1. Recognizes that God is the unique source of all truth, and
2. Relates all truth back to an understanding of God and his purposes for this life and the next.

For the Christian to have a Scriptural worldview, to know the truth, is to know the source of truth, the God of the

Bible. There is no distinction between the two, for to know God by His Son, Jesus Christ, is to accept His truth fully rather than piecemeal. It is to adopt a thoroughly Christian point of view.

So, one asks himself, "Do I have a biblical worldview?" George Barna used these questions in his survey to determine if Americans have a truly Biblical worldview:[16]

1. Do absolute moral truths exist?
2. Is absolute truth defined by the Bible?
3. Did Jesus Christ live a sinless life?
4. Is God the all-powerful and all-knowing Creator of the universe, and does He still rule it today?
5. Is salvation a gift from God that cannot be earned?
6. Is Satan real?
7. Does a Christian have a responsibility to share his or her faith in Christ with other people?
8. Is the Bible accurate in all of its teachings?

Of course, these questions are taken straight from Scripture. Only 4% of Americans reflected a Biblical worldview in answer to these questions. Remarkably only a dismal 9% of so-called "born-again"[17] believers answered all of these questions in the affirmative. Apparently Christians have accepted a hodgepodge of individual truth claims that come from everywhere but the Bible. But what's more important than your "yes" to these questions is whether your life shows it. Granted, we are all sinners and fall short, but most of our gut reactions will reflect what we deep-down, honest-to-goodness believe to be real and true. If we don't really believe the truth of God and live it, then we Christians will be subject to the constant bombardment from television, film, music, newspapers and magazines, the internet, books and academia. Sadly we are corrupted from a Biblical worldview without even knowing it. Our witness within the context of Biblical Christianity then becomes confusing and misleading. We have taken for granted the biblical directive to establish a Christian worldview:

> As you therefore have received Christ Jesus the Lord, so walk in Him, rooted and built up in Him and established in the faith, as you have been taught, abounding in it with thanksgiving. Beware lest anyone cheat you through philosophy and empty deceit, according to the tradition of men, according to the basic principles of the world, and not according to Christ (Col 2:6-8).

If we feed on a smorgasbord of unexamined beliefs our lives are made purposeless and fragmented. If we say that our God, in Jesus, is truth, we would do well to live lives that are based on the truth He has revealed to us in his Word. We should ask the ultimate questions of life from the Scriptures; we should evaluate all other worldviews in the light of the Scripture:[18]

1. Is there a god and what is he like?
2. What is the nature and origin of the universe?
3. What is the nature and origin of man?
4. What happens to man after death?
5. Where does knowledge come from?
6. What is the basis of ethics and morality?
7. What is the meaning of human history?

It is the last question which I wish to examine in Part II. Mature Christians, of all people, should greatly appreciate history realizing that ours is essentially a historical religion. It is a religion whose prime dogmas are based on events. Recording real events in time, historical books make up much of the Bible. Biblical characters lived in real time, not as mythical or legendary figures. The Fall, Flood, Exodus, conquest, Exile, Incarnation, Crucifixion, Resurrection and Ascension occurred in real history. Christianity is thus a thoroughly historical and verifiable faith. This is recognized in the historical approach to apologetics. While men's view of the importance of history changes over time, the believer should recognize the uniqueness of Christianity within the malaise of ideas over the centuries.

PART II
PHILOSOPHY OF HISTORY & CHRISTIAN WORLDVIEW

CHAPTER 3
WHY THE PHILOSOPHY OF HISTORY?

When we think about ultimate purpose as seen in our worldview, we are thinking about cohesiveness in our own lives and the lives of others over time and generations. With the distinct human ability to think about an idea, then think about our thoughts about that idea, we have the makings of metahistory. We have the ability to consider the thought processes surrounding our worldview. These thought processes about worldview are not unlike those surrounding how we do history (historiography) and about how we think about doing history or generational worldview (metahistory).

> *"We are not always clear at the beginning of an action exactly what it is that we are aiming at. We start off in what we hope is the right direction, but can only define our goal as we come nearer."*(Aristotle, Nichomachean Ethics*)*

My modest idea was to contrast the Christian world view with philosophies of history as described by familiar analogies: cyclic, linear, dialectic, evolutionary, and so forth. I found very little in the literature to support the idea. Hayden White's *Metahistory (1973)* was written with the idea that writing history is best described in terms of figures of speech, thus turning historical narrative into forms of literature in order to reveal the historian's *presuppositions.* This changes the conception of history as impartial and *empirical* description into narratives of romance, comedy, tragedy and satire. In other words history becomes literature. This line of thinking follows my own in that a historian inevitably goes into the process with certain *presuppositions* and inclinations. Furthermore, he does not want to be boring in his report. These will color and shape his account though he may present as if it were totally *empirical.* "Totally *empirical,*" of course is possible only in so far as his witnesses are impartial and factually persistent. For example, he might think history cyclical like the seasons or he might believe it to be totally random like Brownian motion. Frank Ankersmit's *History and Tropology (1995) pursued this idea more fully and perhaps debunked it.* Without pursuing all of that subtlety I decided to stick to the basic idea of metaphor as *presupposition* in one's approach to writing and understanding history. A historian by definition presents generalizations, probably organized around his own world view.

I thought it would be helpful to produce a kind of "history of the philosophy of history" by surveying Western Civilization in terms of what had been said about history. This will present a kind of meta-history which has an effect on, or is effected by, what may be called the Christian world view. The Christian world view is specifically that laid out by the Christian Scriptures, God's Word to mankind. Obviously, it is also cultural, generational, provincial and formalized by the Church. The task of presenting these precepts, biases and ways of looking at the world became monumental, so I have truncated my findings and extrapolations sufficiently to retain useful generalizations. Next, I presented eight metaphors for the philosophy of history or *worldview*. Finally, I have outlined a discussion for the impact of Christian worldview on the philosophy of history, and conversely, non-Christian worldviews on Christian historical apologetics. Admittedly, I have slighted Eastern world views, because, other than through the study of comparative religion, I am woefully deficient. Consequently, my generalizations are largely Western.

Hopefully, this discussion brings academia down to the level of common understanding sufficiently to make it interesting reading for the novice. You might call it "a survey of Western historical thinking in contrast to the Christian world view." Its usefulness may be seen in two ways. First, the reader will become aware that his is not the only way of looking at history. He will realize that, in fact, he has a world view. If he does not have a *world view*, he will realize that he is living in confusion. Secondly, he will realize that he must be ready to defend his own *world view*. This is implicit in *apologetics*, in particular with this paper, historical apologetics.

> *Always be ready to give an account of the hope that is within you.* – the Apostle Peter (1 Pet 3:15).

While one may feel the mandate to "always be ready to give an account," the study of history is really motivated by natural curiosity; men are interested in what other men have done. But on some level one could say that it amounts to the search for truth; men want to know who, what, where, when, how and why. They want to understand influence and manipulation. They want to know how their present fits into the past. They want to know if there is a driving force beyond the happenstance of men or whether men act with random volition. They want to know too if there is a grand scheme or purpose. They want to know if history reflects *progress* or simply *change.* Men do history precisely because they are not there to experience it first-hand. The discipline of history advances on two legs: one of them is evidence, the other is interpretation. Out of the historian's findings will come organization of the facts into something intelligible to communicate, often narrative, and less often, broad analysis with implications for progress. What can we draw from the philosophy of history for Christian apologetics, particularly historical apologetics, and more generally, the broad perspective required for a proper defense of the faith? The historical apologist John Warwick Montgomery frames his argument this way:

> *"The perennial dilemma of man (corporate and personal) as to the meaning of existence finds its resolution in Christian revelation. Agreeing with Socrates' pronouncement that "the unexamined life is not worth living," examination is called for as to the meaning of history, ethical values, and the significance of human life. If history is a 'tale told by an idiot, signifying nothing' (Shakespeare), or, less elegantly, 'bunk' and 'the succession of one damned thing after the other' (Henry Ford), then historical action loses all significance." Value systems must be more than arbitrary, otherwise they will contradict one another and produce no transcendent human rights.*[19]

Why is it important for Christians to involve themselves with historical overview and to question what has been written? The subject of the philosophy of history has relevance particularly to historical apologetics, which stresses beginning with historical evidence for the truth of Christianity. The resurrection of Christ is obviously the linchpin. Beyond this, what part does the fulfillment of

26

prophecy, the preservation of the scriptural text, or witness of the historical church, for example, play in apologetics? What witness does history itself give to the historical Jesus? Of course, the prevailing Christian doctrine regarding matters of faith is based in the "*Sola Scriptura*" of our credo. While the divine-human text gives us all that is necessary to salvation, all that we need to know on this side of heaven regarding matters of faith, the Bible itself provides a reliable history and perspective of history. While its insights guide our thoughts, there is much to be gained from a broad historical perspective in understanding worldviews. From where, other than the Bible, do our Christian worldviews come? Is our own Christian worldview tainted or adversely influenced by secular worldviews? How does our "worldliness" effect our interpretation of the biblical history? Conversely, how does the biblical perspective affect our broad view of life, politics and popular culture? How does the exegetical and hermeneutical mandate constrain our view of history? As Christians, have we taken personally God's purpose and design? Do we see Him at work in history as well as in nature (perhaps, there is no difference)?

In what is usually called "the **Speculative Philosophy of History**" (*Meta-history*), that branch of philosophy concerned with questions about the meaningfulness of history and the nature of historical explanation, we will playfully consider differing explanations of history in terms of selected metaphors or analogies (See Chapter 4).

Another branch may be called "the **Analytic *Philosophy of history*** (*Historiography*), which rose to prominence only in the 20th century, and focuses on the methods by which practicing historians treat the human past. Scientific method, probability theory and textual criticism have more and more to say about the process. The historiographer develops rules for investigation, collection and historical reporting based upon established criteria for doing history. Being "scientific" has not kept the historiographer from error of assumption. Witness computer assisted efforts to establish "true," underlying authorship and provenience of New Testament writings. Montgomery relates this story:

MacGregor and Morton fed the "literary style" of Romans and Galatians into a computer, so as to compare them with the other New Testament letters claiming to be Pauline; their conclusion: none of these other works were written by Paul. Then the MacGregor and Morton book on the subject was itself subjected to computer analysis using parallel criteria, proving that their work was actually a product of multiple authorship. Style and vocabulary are not sufficiently stable criteria for determining questions of authorship.[20]

Another example of possible errant "science" is the textual criticism of Wescott and Hort who formalized a New Testament Greek Text (1881-82) which pronounced the older textual fragments in recovery of the New Testament to be more genuine due to the likelihood of less tampering. This led to wholesale acceptance of their "critical" Greek text over the "Textus Receptus" of Erasmus, Stephanus and Beza (of the historical church). What irony if the very few texts on which Wescott and Hort built their work (codex's Vaticanus, Sinaiticus and Alexandrinus) were themselves tampered with in earlier centuries!

Barzun & Graff, in their classic manual on all aspects of research and writing, deal with historiography in terms of the searcher's virtues. Understanding that history is a joint product of nature and culture, it is important to understand from where the writer is coming. There are certain virtues that can be valued in the research and writing of history:[21]

1. **Accuracy**: If history is the story of past facts, those facts must be ascertained accurately, steadily and religiously. The historian must pursue precision and exactitude in-so-far as possible.
2. **The Love of Order**: There is in any piece of research so much to be read, noted down, compared, verified, indexed, grouped, organized, and recopied, that unless one is capable of adhering to a system, the chances of error grow alarmingly.
3. **Logic**: This is related to order, but different. Ideas must flow from one another, build precept upon precept, detail to generalization.
4. **Honesty**: Unless you put down what you find to be true with complete candor, you are nullifying the very result you aim at, which is the discovery of the past as embedded in records. Hypotheses are to be abandoned as reality is uncovered.
5. **Self-Awareness**: The historian must not only be honest but make his standards of judgment plain, and thus lessen the influence of personal bias.
6. **Imagination**: The researcher must again and again imagine the kind of source he would like to have before he can find it. To be sure, it may not exist; but if it does, its whereabouts must be presumed in order to increase the likelihood of finding it.

How one approaches the study of history reveals a great deal about his worldview. Some view history as fine drama; others view it as cyclic repetition, others as evolution and progress, others as a struggle between the classes and means of production; some view it as the critical analysis of sources and probabilities, others more cynical as the propaganda of the winners, and some as random occurrence without predictive value. Most Christians see history as providential *eschatology*. Among these views are certain contradictions and irrationalities which we shall consider. In any case ones view of history reveals his worldview.

It is important for a Christian to be consistent in his worldview if he is to be effective in his defense of the faith. For example, can a Christian simultaneously hold that "nothing ever changes" and that "we are being transformed from glory into glory," or that great and momentous things will happen on "The Day of the Lord?" Can he use the popular phrase "What goes around comes around" (which is nothing but Hindu karma) and also hold that "in this world you will have trouble. But take heart! I have overcome the world"? That doesn't sound like karma. If we are equally impacted by popular culture, academic pronouncements of every kind and biblical teaching, if we consider them of equal import and hold "that there is a little truth in everything," then we are inevitably confused about what we believe. I am attempting here to discuss this challenge in terms of the philosophy of history and thus shed light on the Christian. Allow me to requote John Byle who is mentioned in Chapter 1:

All worldviews are based on presuppositions, on basic initial assumptions about reality that are rarely stated explicitly. Such worldview presuppositions set our standards for what we consider to be reasonable. Different worldviews may entail radically different views of rationality. Nevertheless, conflicting worldviews can usually be assessed in terms of quite general criteria such as consistency, experience, and livability. Any viable worldview must be able to accommodate the basic common sense notions needed for normal conversation and scientific activity. In particular, we stressed the necessity of truth and logic, as well as the importance of the principle of sufficient reason. Embracing a worldview is not a dry academic exercise. Our worldview sets the direction for our life. It determines the path we follow and the goals we seek. It guides us in deciding how to live our lives. Our answers to worldview questions are matters of life and death.[22]

The whole discussion of the philosophy of history longs for a grand design *(Cosmology)* behind historical forces. Does the study of history show design, or is it quite random? Why do we do history? What purpose for mankind is implied in the process and where is this all leading *(Teleology)*?

Michael Stanford opines, "*Purpose seems to account for some major historical occurrences, like the post-Hegira spread of Islam, the Crusades, the Renaissance, the Reformation, the Enlightenment and the abolition of slave trade. In none of these cases did things turn out exactly as intended, yet they would never have happened at all had not many people at the same time had a common intention. It seems that there is a at least some room for teleological explanation in history*".[23]

But, does history reveal purpose or goals on the part of a Grand Design, whether theistic or naturalistic? Does history present a linear sequence of progress? Are there recurrent cycles? Some have said there is no overriding organization or logical order to history. Others have emphasized the importance of contingency and chance in the playing out of events. Can the past help us predict the future? Many who have concerned themselves with questions about the nature of historical knowledge *(Historical Epistemology)* and interpretation of the past have spent a good deal of time studying the history of various historical concepts and ideas; and in doing so some have concluded that there are no absolute ideals of historical method or truth which can be isolated from their own peculiar historical and social contexts. This is the problem of *Historicism*. To gain a broader perspective we ask, "What have the great thinkers said or implied about these questions down through the ages?"

CHAPTER 4
A RIDICULOUSLY SHORT HISTORY OF THE PHILOSOPHY OF HISTORY

Following a chronological and thematic history of western civilization and Christianity it is possible to identify trends, great innovative thought and leadership, as well as sea-changes in popular culture. These great themes imply, if not express directly, the changing views of history. The great questions are "What drives history?" "What can be learned from history?" and "Who controls or writes history?" These questions are inextricable from religious and secular belief systems, from political and religious institutions and from local utterance as well as broad philosophical thought. How is history collected? Stanford, in his discussion of *historicity* described the difficulty:

> *Looking at the past is rather like standing in a dense crowd to watch a spectacle. One never has a clear, uninterrupted view, but has the heads in the crowd in front move, so one sees different parts of the scene.*[24]

Of course, in our generalizations we are scarcely dealing with the complexity of it all, rational and mysterious, patterned or unpredictable. Life and thought are "messy" from any immediate vantage point. The following is my poor attempt to gain perspective from broad historical reference. Extrapolations are highlighted and underlined:

PREHISTORIC SOCIETIES leave us little or no evidence of how they thought about history. One of the most intriguing movies I have ever seen, "The Gods Must Be Crazy" (1980), centers around Xi, who is part of an isolated tribe in Botswana with no knowledge of the world beyond. One day, a Coca-Cola bottle is thrown out of an airplane and falls to earth unbroken. Initially, this strange artifact seems to be a "gift" from the gods. Xi's people find many uses for it including everything from a toy to an object of worship. Of course, there is only one glass bottle to go around. Children play with it, women use it to help in food preparation, men fight over its ownership and someone kills another by hitting him over the head with it. Xi decides that the bottle is an evil thing and must be thrown off the "end of the earth," which for Xi is the top of a cliff with a solid layer of low-lying clouds obscuring the landscape below. This convinces Xi that he has reached the edge of the world, and he throws the bottle off the cliff and returns to his tribe and a warm welcome from his family. The hunters and gatherers of prehistory undoubtedly had their own history carried along by their shared language, but the groups of people tended to be smaller and their languages more fragile. The ability to think inter-culturally, let alone develop what may be called a "history," would depend on exploration, communication and education. We can only speculate what men thought as we examine something of what they did, but we have little evidence beyond that implied by archeological and anthropological findings.

One characteristic of humanity is our extraordinary capacity for dealing with symbols. God created us with the ability to understand and create language, or we never could have known the Word or the Word made flesh (John 1:14).[25]

A society's own sense of history would depend upon its developed language:

As well as being the banners and ensigns of human groups, languages guard our memories too. Even when they are unwritten, languages are the most powerful tools we have to conserve our past knowledge, transmitting it, ever and anon, to the next generation. Any human language binds together a human community, by giving it a network of communication; but it also dramatizes it, providing the means to tell, and to remember, its stories.[26]

The **ANCIENT HEBREWS**, a well-traveled nation, present a worldview that is at least multi-cultural. Its prehistory is captured in oral tradition, thought to have later been written by **Moses** (c.1520-1407 BC). This <u>history of God's interaction with a nation</u> made universal assertions toward a mankind with common opportunity for salvation by faith. God promised through Abraham that *"all nations would be blessed."* Furthermore, it was made clear that it <u>was not only for the Hebrews but for all men that God provided salvation and revelation</u>. That revelation would be not only of Himself, but of man and his nature, of the nature of depravity and the value of life. In all of this is the faithful oversight of a providential God who is not capricious and who has the welfare of all humanity in mind. It seems unlikely that such a universal system of hope and salvation would be conceived by the Hebrews for their own benefit alone. Witness Solomon's dedicatory prayer for the new temple (957 BC):

"Also concerning the foreigner who is not from Thy people Israel, when he comes from a far country for Thy great name's sake and Thy mighty hand and Thine outstretched arm, when they come and pray toward this house, then hear Thou from heaven, from Thy dwelling place, and do according to all for which the foreigner calls to Thee, in

order that all the peoples of the earth may know Thy name, and fear Thee, as do Thy people Israel, and that they may know that this house which I have built is called by Thy name" (2 Chron 6:32-33).

The **PRE-CLASSICAL** epic poetry of **Homer** (fl.850 BC) in *The Iliad & The Odyssey* show ancient Greek use of literature as philosophical expression. **Herodotus** (c.484-420 BC) is known as the "father of history." He chronicled the war between Greece and Persia. Though he loved a good story, he clearly <u>distinguished in his history between what was based on hearsay and what he had seen and heard personally or had learned by inquiry.</u>[27]

Thucydides (c.460-395 BC), noted for his account of the Peloponnesian War, described <u>history as *"Philosophy teaching by examples.*</u>" **Plato** (c.427-347 BC) saw reality as the "forms" which had their existence outside of the material world. The implications for the enterprise of meta-history are that <u>design and purpose are discoverable outside the observed world.</u> **Aristotle** (384-322 BC) saw reality as discoverable through observation of the material world; the essence of things was understood empirically. The <u>implications for historiography are enormous in that greater effort must be taken in the collection of data and that no large conclusions can be drawn without the presence of sufficient data.</u>

The remarkable contribution of the ancient **ROMANS** to historical thinking undoubtedly is the formalization of Law across cultural boundaries and the success of the Pax Romana. Not ignoring the significance of the widespread use of Latin, a unifying phenomenon in itself, the implications for history are that <u>there are identifiable universals for justice and that historical interpretation involves more than provincial arbitration.</u>

The **FIRST CHRISTIANS,** though they were influenced by the Classical World, inherited the Hebrew worldview outlined above. At first Jesus Christ was seen incompletely by His followers as a political savior ("He came to His own and they knew Him not"). But Jesus, whose "kingdom was not of this world" brought to them a divine perspective. For the first Christians history was a product of God's intervention; history became more than that of the Hebrew nation, but a divine *eschatology*. What was written through man by God's inspiration was more than the logos derived from Greek Stoicism; it was the last and over-riding Word of God (THE LOGOS of "I AM THAT I AM"). History, both as written by Moses the Lawgiver, the Scribes who faithfully brought to remembrance God's dealing with their ancestors, the Prophets who spoke for God and the Poets who communicated with and about their God, together with the Gospel, Luke's Acts of the Apostles, circulated correspondence (epistles) and John's Revelation of the Christ, now became a history which brought explanation of God's purpose for humanity. This *teleology* indicated that a phenomenon is to be explained or understood in terms of its consequences, not merely its causes. The study of the end or purpose of things is usually taken to involve a mind that has such intentions or purposes. For Christians this was the *Logos.*

The Christian apologist, **Justin Martyr** (c.AD100-165), made clear that Christianity is the all-embracing Truth. Truth concerning existence, wherever it appears, is Christian truth; there cannot be truth anywhere which is not in principle included in Christian truth. "The Logos appeared full of grace and truth" (Fourth Gospel). He is the full Logos of God Himself. Christianity is not merely the best religion; it is the negation of all religions. Christ is universal in embracing all mankind, all classes, groups and social stratifications of mankind. <u>History, like the truth of the Gospel, is for the masses</u>.

Conversely, the early apologists had to defend Christianity against the philosophers and emperors who would make it exclusive. The **GNOSTICS** taught that only by participation in the divine could Christianity be understood; it was mysterious and unreachable to non-participants. As mystical communion, it did not yield to analysis and synthetic research. This influence brought a renewal of ancient mystery traditions, the psychic and magical elements which appeared in the religious propaganda of the East. The trend was already being fought in the early Church as revealed in the letters of Paul. <u>Implications for history were that the created world was evil by nature; you cannot trust what you see and touch</u>. Salvation was thought to be liberation from materialism.

> *There is no place for eschatology in this dualistic worldview, for the end of the world is seen in the light of dualism. A dualistic fulfillment is not a fulfillment; it implies a split in God himself.*[28]

In the end Greek philosophy reached a state in which philosophy had become religion, and religion had become a mystical philosophy. After the Egyptian born **Plotinus** (AD205-270), the Neo-Platonists **Clement** (fl. 202-230) and **Origen** (185-254) of Alexandria would promote this spirit-body dualism in the elevation of Christianity as the highest form of education. Though Scripture was considered the ultimate authority, its nature was thought to be mystical. <u>Scripture and History were best taught as allegory</u>.

With the **CHRISTIAN ROMAN EMPIRE** (312-590) the Medieval church father, **AUGUSTIN** (354-430), *The City of God*, taught YAHWEH as Lord of History in the context of "cosmic combat." History was understood as the embattled trace of God's ultimate sovereignty.

THE MIDDLE AGES (590-1570) found Europe in transition after the fall of the Roman Empire and weakening of the papacy. An agonizing Rome recovering from the tragedies of floods, the atrocities of war and the relentless spread of the plague, enlisted Celtic and Benedictine monks to serve as a spiritual militia to win the barbarians of Europe to the Christian faith. In his book, *Pastoral Care*, **Gregory the Great** (fl. 600 AD) stressed the balance of emulating the example of "Christ Our Lord in continued prayer on the mountain" (not forgetting the inner life of the soul) while also doing "miracles in the cities (mingling in sympathy with the necessities of the infirmed)." Out of his reticent leadership and his appointment by Emperor Justin as prefect of Rome, the city was transformed from that of Caesars to the city of popes. Through Pope Gregory's missionary zeal, out of the ashes of ruin, grew a unified Roman Catholic Europe. Typical among the Medieval monks and priests writing in Latin was the Venerable Bede (c.673-735), described as "the father of English history." He consciously attempted to distinguish between fact and rumor. His Ecclesiastical History of the English People, however, freely identified God's providential hand repeatedly intervening in history, sometimes performing miracles.

Charlemagne (c.742-814) and the French alliance with the papacy affected the course of European politics and Christianity for centuries. He formed the first European empire since that of the Roman Caesars. Beyond his military conquests, Charlemagne through the palaces and monasteries of Europe fostered a revival of learning and the arts leaving a cultural heritage that later generations could build upon. With the later decline into feudalism the **Holy Roman Empire** still had its impact in two important principles:

1) In the loyalties of men, the spiritual has the primacy over the secular, and
2) The families of men can find true unity only in Christ and in obedience to the law of God.

The popes may not have understood that Christianity's highest satisfactions are not guaranteed by possession of special places, and the sword is never God's way to extend Christ's church. This fault assured the religious collapse of the whole structure.[29]

The ability of emperors and popes, no matter how high-principled their intentions to force the outcome of world history, was short-lived. The on-going controversy was "Did the Pope have authority over the King or the King over the Pope?" In the context of such struggle, one characteristic of mankind is its ability to back away from its immediate circumstance and view the larger picture. Men seek through historical investigation to rediscover themselves within the context of their ancestors and find value in remembering.

The stream of time, irresistible, ever moving, carries off and bears away all things that come to birth and plunges them into utter darkness, both deeds of no account and deeds which are mighty and worthy of commemoration; as the playwright [Sophocles] says, it "brings to light that which was unseen and shrouds from us that which was manifest." Nevertheless, the science of History is a great bulwark against the stream of Time; in a way it checks this irresistible flood, it holds in a tight grasp whatever it can seize floating on the surface and will not allow it to slip away into the depths of Oblivion." (Anna Comnena (1083-1153) The Alexiad.)

Such effort to rediscover the past led to what historians term "**SCHOLASTICISM**." **Anselm of Canterbury,** (1033-1109) like all scholastics, asserted that in the Holy Scriptures, and in their interpretation by the fathers, all truth is directly or indirectly enclosed. It was *"credo ut intelligam"* (I believe in order to understand, not I understand in order to believe). <u>Faith was not an individual act but participation in a living tradition. In a sense, faith was participation in history</u>. Specifically, the content of eternal truth, of principles of truth, is grasped by the subjection of our will to the Christian message and the consequent experience arising from this subjection. <u>Doing history, then, is motivated by the faith experience</u>.

In the fervor of "Scholasticism" the brilliant Dominican monk **Thomas Aquinas** (1225-1274) was dispatched to Paris from Italy in an effort to curb the negative impact of Greek and Eastern philosophies on Christianity. His *Summa Theologica* examined these writings point by point, refuting some and reconciling others with Christianity. He made a clear distinction between philosophy and theology, reason and revelation; without contradiction; both come from the same God. Aquinas taught that thanks to the work of Christ and the meritorious deeds of the saints, the church has access to a "treasury of merit" - a great spiritual reservoir.

Scholastic theology may have gone too far, claimed too much for itself and for the church. A clue to the heights of arrogance lies in Innocent III's claim that the pope is the judge of the world, "set in the midst between God and man." As such <u>the Church would be the lone repository of historical interpretation</u>.

The 14th Century saw a decline in papal authority; the people no longer accepted papal interference in what they regarded as purely political matters. Boniface was not a beloved pope, and was widely criticized. **Dante** (1265-1321), the Italian genius who wrote *The Divine_Comedy*, reserved a place in hell for Boniface. Thus even men in the early 14th Century distinguished between religious and secular authority and recognized the rights of each in its own place. Men began to think in terms of "national churches," and the church governed by representative bodies. The English theologian **John Wycliffe** (c.1328-1384) anticipated the Protestant Reformation in his rejection of the biblical basis for the papacy and for transubstantiation of the communion host. The Czech reformer **John Hus** (c.1372-1415) was excommunicated for attacking the corruption of the clergy.

The **ITALIAN RENAISSANCE** of the <u>15th century</u> represented a reconnection of the West with <u>classical antiquity</u>, the absorption of knowledge, particularly <u>mathematics</u> from <u>Arabic</u>, the return of experimentalism, the focus on the importance of living well in the present (<u>Renaissance humanism</u>), an explosion of the dissemination of knowledge brought on by <u>printing</u> and the creation of new techniques in <u>art</u>, <u>poetry</u> and <u>architecture</u>, leading in turn to a radical change in the style and substance of the <u>arts and letters</u>. This period represents Europe emerging from a long period of stagnancy, and the rise of <u>commerce</u> and <u>exploration</u>. As Renaissance Humanism moved through Europe there arose new hope for a better society as represented by **Thomas More**'s (1478-1535) political essay <u>Utopia</u> (1516). To ask people to think of a better world, of refashioning (if not revolutionizing) their economy, social structure, and value-systems, is to invite them to <u>see their</u> <u>future history as a reservoir of possibilities for their own</u> <u>conscious manipulation.</u> No longer would their preconception be that history was "a monotony of ultimately insignificant happenings from which nothing can be learnt". More was beheaded for refusing to recognize Henry VIII's authority over the Pope. Nationalism also increased as the papacy weakened. **Niccolo Machiavelli** (1469-1527) is known for his treatise on political expediency, *The Prince* (1513). It is widely regarded as one of the basic texts of Western political science, and represents a basic change in the attitude and image of government.

> *You must know there are two ways of contesting, the one by the law, the other by force; the first method is proper to men, the second to beasts; but because the first is frequently not sufficient, it is necessary to have recourse to the second. Therefore it is necessary for a prince to understand how to avail himself of the beast and the man.*[30]

Whatever the form of government, Machiavelli held, only success and glory really matter. <u>History is by the victors.</u> <u>There is a "connectedness" of history from which we can</u> <u>learn lessons, guidelines and principles.</u> There is no inclusion of God as a driving force in history for Machiavelli.

THE EMERGENCE OF PRINTING had a huge impact in disseminating the <u>secularism, individualism and cultural</u> <u>relativism</u> of the Renaissance. The new medium first made widespread the criticism of the Universal Church from cultured, respected figures such as **Desiderius Erasmus** (1467-1536), *The Praise of Folly* (1509), early in the 16th C., and then enabled a veritable explosion of highly charged pamphleteering which fueled the Protestant Reformation from the 1520's onward. Systematic censorship of books arose simultaneously. Both church and state drew up lists of prohibited writings, continually revised and updated, so that "the sword" was applied to "the pen." Ironically, <u>history making was enabled by printing and potentially disabled by censorship</u>. However, censorship did not succeed.

Martin Luther (1483-1546), an Augustinian monk, presented the real breakthrough for which there was no compromise with Roman Catholicism. The Roman system was one of divine-human authority, represented and actualized by ecclesiastical management. The system was objective, not personal; quantitative, not qualitative; relative and conditioned, not absolute. But Luther realized that the relation to God was personal faith. Either he is separated from God or he is not. There are no gradual degrees of separation in Luther's mind. **THE REFORMATION** (Protestantism) restated the unconditional categories of the Bible. The magical and legal elements disappear, for grace is a personal communion of God with the sinner. Repentance was not a single act; penitence was the whole life of the believer. The only works of satisfaction are works of love; all other works are an arbitrary invention of the church. Salvation is by grace and through faith, the reverse of faith in the mystical and dependence on the grace of the church. Luther rejected this impersonal participation in the sacraments, for they are not the grace that saves you. Transubstantiation was destroyed and the sacramental foundation of the whole hierarchical system was removed. The Mass, which was viewed as a sacrifice to God, was a blasphemy and sacrilege to Luther who saw man as having nothing to bring to God. Men should instead expect the gift of God himself in Christ. One can say that Roman Catholicism was marketing eternal life. A man could buy indulgences and in this way get rid of the punishments of earth and purgatory. Luther hoped to reform the church in placing his **"Ninety-Five Theses"** on the door of the Wittenberg church (1517). Luther accepted the God-ordained power of the state to administrate the church; he did not believe in revolution as such, for it contradicted God's destiny. The objection is that this set up an atmosphere for outrageous government such as Nazi Germany, but he like Hegel saw the state as organized society repressing sin and preventing chaos. Nevertheless, one can make the connection in speculating why the church did not "stand up to" evil despotism. This is an extreme view of <u>God's providence in history</u>. **John Calvin** (1509-1564), a Swiss protestant theologian, gave many more functions to the state than did Luther. Theocracy had to be established, known for his *Institutes of the Christian Religion* (1536), the rule of God through the application of evangelical laws in the political situation. This was a reasoned extension of Calvin's emphasis on God's sovereignty. <u>History would reveal but the footprints of God</u>.

Political theory remained moribund, bound up with the immediacy of events. The French political writer, **Jean Bodin** (1529-1596) set down principles to demonstrate the need for any society to be governed by a sovereign power, without which any state would lose its unity and relapse into the threatening anarchy of unchecked families at war with each other. He drew from <u>the example of Roman law which required rules for historical interpretation.</u>

Eventually, the **ENLIGHTENMENT** and the **AGE OF REASON** sprang from the soil of a new faith in law and order. Modern science arose in the sixteenth and seventeenth centuries and filled men with visions of a new day of peace and harmony. These pioneers of modern science forced men to think in a new way about the universe: **Copernicus** (1473-1543), who insisted that the sun, not the earth, was the center of our universe; **Johann Kepler** (1571-1630), who concluded that the sun emitted a magnetic force that moved the planets in their courses, and **Galileo Galilei** (1564-1642), who proved that the acceleration of falling bodies was constant and made a telescope to examine the planets. Galileo asserted that <u>where the indisputable truths uncovered by science conflicted with the word of God in the Scriptures, then the former should prevail, since words (even those inspired by God) are subject to the limited power of human understanding</u>, as well as often being ambiguous in meaning. Galileo was imprisoned by the Inquisition for advocating heliocentricity. **Francis Bacon** (1561-1626) proposed the "inductive method."

> *For, as many imaginary theories of the heavens can be deduced from the phenomena of the sky, so it is even more easy to found many dogmas upon the phenomena of philosophy; and the plot of this our theatre resembles those of the poetical, where the plots which are invented for the stage are more consistent, elegant, and pleasurable than those taken from real history.*[31]

The rationalist **Rene Descartes** (1596-1650) began by doubting anything that could not be proven through deductive reasoning. **Thomas Hobbes** (1588-1679) asserted that true "philosophical/scientific" ideas are solely the product of logical propositional reasoning. We cannot use what the Bible says about God (or much else) as the basis for discovering truth, for as Hobbes said, "<u>the words under discussion are not the propositions of people philosophizing but the actions of those who pay homage</u>."

All of the discoveries of the Enlightenment had to be united in one all-embracing principle that would explain the motion of bodies in the heavens and present the universe as one great machine operating according to unalterable laws. This was the feat of the most illustrious scientist of the Age of Reason, **Isaac Newton** (1642-1727). In 1687 Newton published his momentous work, *Mathematical Principles of Natural Philosophy*, in which all laws of motion, in the heavens and on the earth, were harmonized in a master principle for the universe, the law of gravitation. The medieval world of unseen spirits – angels and demons – could now be dismissed as superstition. In its place moved a universe subject to physical laws expressed in mathematical symbols. The European Enlightenment represented by Isaac Newton's mechanistic universe implied that the world could be understood without recourse to religion or God. What followed was the application of this mechanistic model to every area including economics, politics and ethics. All were seen as rational, predictable and manipulatable. When this notion was applied to history, _history was seen as operating under certain natural laws and that God had no intervening authority in its operations_. **Alexander Pope** (1688-1744) wrote:

Nature and Nature's laws lay hid in night; God said,
"Let Newton be!" and all was light.

John Locke (1632-1704), in his *"Essay Concerning Human Understanding,"* not only showed how reason functions, but indicated the existence of God as _"the most obvious truth that reason discovers."_ Revelation, itself, for Locke showed Christianity's reasonable character. Belief in Jesus as Messiah and man's ethical behavior are all that Jesus and the apostles required for righteousness. Both of these are basically rational.

Giambattista Vico's (1668-1744) humanism led him to believe that there is a "master key" to understanding history, a distinctive historical stage through which all human institutions have passed, a common principle of humanity (hinting at identifiable patterns in history). He believed that there is a greater affinity between social law and history than between science and history. Meaning and purpose were higher considerations for humanity than causation and "natural law". Traditional categories of knowledge, logical deduction or sense experience, are insufficient. To these must be added a third, the reconstructive imagination or empathetic insight.

The **DIESM** of **Voltaire** (1694-1778), *Candide*, saw God's relationship to the world as a perfect "watchmaker." After having made the watch and wound it up, there would be no need for God to later interfere. The deists rejected miracles and special revelation. Voltaire achieved his greatest fame as the most relentless critic of the established churches, Protestant and Catholic alike. His aim was not religious destruction. He once said that *"if God did not exist, it would be necessary to invent one."* The deists' aim was the destruction of the citadel. **Bishop Joseph Butler** (1692-1752) in his monumental work, *The Analogy of Religion*, virtually ended the debate for thinking people. The deists, with their confident optimism, assumed that they knew all about God's wisdom and purpose. They read it all in the pattern of nature. Butler, however, saw with disarming clarity that life is filled with perplexities and enigmas. He did not try to prove the existence of God. Deists never denied this premise. Nor did he reject reason; he accepted it as man's natural light. But he did challenge reason's sovereignty. *"Reason,"* said Butler, *"provides no complete system of*

knowledge, and in ordinary life it can offer us only probabilities."
Thus, Butler undermined deism's fortress, its confidence in
reason.

In *The Social Contract* **Jean Jacques Rousseau** (1712-1778)
declared that the individual is essentially good but corrupted
by society.

> *In order to discover the rules of society best suited to
> nations, a superior intelligence beholding all the passions
> of men without experiencing any of them would be
> needed. This intelligence would have to be wholly
> unrelated to our nature, while knowing it through and
> through; its happiness would have to be independent of us,
> and yet ready to occupy itself with ours; and lastly, it
> would have, in the march of time, to look forward to a
> distant glory, and, working in one century, to be able to
> enjoy in the next. It would take gods to give men laws.*[32]

A.R.J. Turgot (1727-1781), passionately believed in
progress measured by, and dependent upon, the extent to
which mankind could become ever more "civilized" through
applying "reason" to achieve the fully happy life. All
knowledge was dependent upon the gradual uncovering of
reality through observation, comparison and experiment.
Marquis de Condorcet (1743-1794), known for his work on
the theory of probability, was greatly influenced by Turgot
and built upon the idea of reasoned progress in his "ten
stages of history." For **Edmund Burke** (1729-1797 the
notion of a "history of humankind" was a nonsensical
rationalist abstraction. The only generalization that could
be made was that of change. It is not always progress when
things change for a society. Men cannot manipulate the
present after studying the past, because one's close
proximity makes it impossible to see and understand the

complexity. History is filled with unintended consequences man could not control. It is only chartable after the event. History thus tells us nothing. But in another sense – that of attaining what is possible – it tells us everything. But the British historian, **Edward Gibbon** (1737-1794), would imply the lessons of history through his work, *Decline and Fall of the Roman Empire.*

> *I have but one lamp by which my feet are guided, and that is the lamp of experience. I know no way of judging of the future but by the past* (Patrick Henry, 1736-1799). [33]

Immanuel Kant (1724-1804) saw history as the record of human progress toward rationality and freedom. He confronted the problem of making sense of human history:

> *The only way out for the philosopher, since he cannot assume that mankind follows any rational purpose of its own in its collective actions, is for him to attempt to discover a purpose in nature behind this senseless course of human events, and decide whether it is after all possible to formulate in terms of a definite plan of nature a history of creatures who act without a plan of their own.*[34]

For Kant reason was the means by which the phenomena of experience are translated into understanding. There is Moral Law and the possibility of a world society of "perpetual peace." Although Kant's suggestion of non-divine purposive power behind history was to be taken up in various ways by such other Germans as Hegel and Marx, the idea now finds as little favor with historians as the corresponding notion does with biologists.

For many of the world's great thinkers, whether, poet, playwright, philosopher, political theorist or historian, the writing of history was impossibly bound up with the need to persuade for ones own purposes, particularly for the sake of nation building. **Johann Wolfgang von Goethe** (1749-1832), the author of *Faust*, would comment, "Patriotism ruins history." **Georg Wilhelm Friedrich Hegel** (1770-1831), not without his own idealistic agenda, would say that history is a "slaughter bench." The State is the "march of God upon the earth." Hegel proclaimed a "World Spirit of Reason," immanently working in history, bringing mankind to an idealistic goal of freedom by way of world-historical epochs, the last of which would be the German.

Arthur Schopenhauer (1788-1860) author of *The World As Will and Representation*, saw history quite differently; he wrote:

> Hence arises the fact that everything better struggles through only with difficulty, becomes effective, or meets with a hearing, but the absurd and perverse in the realm of thought, the dull and tasteless in the sphere of art, and the wicked and fraudulent in the sphere of action, really assert a supremacy that is disturbed only by brief interruptions.[35]

Leopold von Ranke (1795-1886), *The History of the Popes*, the greatest historian of his time, wrote that "every epoch is immediate to God, and its worth... rests in its own existence, its own self." Meanwhile the demon of "relativism" reared its head in the philosophy of **Hegel**, the idea that knowledge is strictly limited by the nation and epoch of the knower. He would feed the mind of Marx in his realization that each nation rises to prominence, dies, and then becomes the fodder for growth of the next.

Karl Marx (1818-1883), *Das Kapital*, took "dialectic," that concept in Plato and Kant of thesis antithesis-synthesis, and retooled it in a materialistic manner. In *The Communist Manifesto*, his collaboration with **Friedrich Engels** (1820-1895), he made "**DIALECTIC MATERIALISM**" apply to civilizations, giving it a prominent role in world history. It was portrayed as a progressive struggle between the classes for control of the means of production which would inevitably lead to a synthesis of social justice under communism. Later the Russian revolutionary **Leon Trotsky** (1879-1940) would pick up on the theme in his encouraging the development of socialist economic policy whereby production and distribution of goods are owned collectively and a single-party government centrally controls the economy working toward a social order in which all goods are equally shared. He would be banished by Stalin in1929. The governments under such pretense of controlled altruism, ironically, have become some of the most godless and vicious dictatorships in recent history. Consider the unintended consequences for history based on the sincerest of intentions.

The monumental historical novel *War and Peace*, **Leo Tolstoy** (1828-1910), contains a wonderful piece of historiography he calls "*The Second Epilogue*." Here are a few of its statements:[36]

- *History is the life of nations and of humanity. To seize and put into words, to describe directly the life of humanity or even of a single nation, appears impossible.*
- *At the basis of the works of all the modern historians from Gibbon to Buckle, despite their seeming disagreements and the apparent novelty of their outlooks, like those two old, unavoidable assumptions, (1) that nations are guided by*

individual men, and (2) the existence of a known aim to which these nations and humanity at large are tending.

- If instead of a divine power some other force has appeared, it should be explained in what this new force consists, for the whole interest of history lies precisely in that force.

- History seems to assume that this force is self-evident and known to everyone. But in spite of every desire to regard it as known, anyone reading many historical works cannot help doubting whether this new force, so variously understood by the historians themselves, is really quite well known to everybody.

- What force moves nations? Writers of universal history who deal with all the nations seem to recognize how erroneous is the specialist historians' view of the force which produces events. They do not recognize it as a power inherent in heroes and rulers, but as the resultant of a multiplicity of variously directed forces. In describing a war or the subjugation of a people, a general historian looks for the cause of the event not in the power of one man, but in the interaction of many persons connected with the event.

- The theory of the transference of the collective will of the people to historic persons may perhaps explain much in the domain of jurisprudence and be essential for its purposes, but in its application to history, as soon as revolutions, conquest, or civil wars occur – that is, as soon as history begins – that theory explains nothing. The theory seems irrefutable just because the act of transference of the people's will cannot be verified, for it never occurred.

- Only the expression of the will of the Deity, not dependent on time, can relate to a whole series of events occurring over a period of years or centuries, and only the Deity, independent of everything, can by His sole will determine *the direction of humanity's movement; but man acts in time and himself takes part in what occurs.*

Although it is more characteristic of Eastern philosophies of history to involve a cyclical rather than a linear pattern, it is not unheard of in Western historical thinking. **Oswald Spengler** (1880-1936), *The Decline of the West* argued that history moves in cyclical patterns, and that self-contained human cultures follow a life cycle similar to that of living organisms and nature; thus a culture develops from barbarism to a civilized classical period, and finally stagnates, decays, and dies in a new barbarism of hyper-commercialism. **Arnold Toynbee** (1889-1975), another cyclical historian and system builder, analyzing 34 civilizations, believed that culture cycles respond to lead to mature higher religions, and ultimately, to the Kingdom of God.

> *The goals they set for history (Kant's reason, Hegel's freedom, Marx's classless society, Toynbee's ecumenical civilization) cannot be demonstrated to have a necessitarian character about them. In choosing their respective goals, the secular philosophers of history continually make judgments as to what is significant and what is valuable (Hegel's idealism, Marx's materialism, Spengler's favouring of instinct and the agrarian society); but in no case are they able to justify these value judgments in absolute terms. These philosophers gratuitously presuppose ethical principles (Hegel's exempting of history's "great men" from the ordinary standards of right and wrong, Marx's willingness to let the end justify the means in bringing about the classless society through revolution). Secular and humanistic historical searchlights are incapable of illuminating all of*

the path we have traversed, and they continually meet a wall of fog ahead.[37]

In his "An Enquiry Concerning Human Understanding," **David Hume** (1711-1776), had already asserted that human knowledge comes from sense experience. Consequently, he denied the validity of all abstract ideas, including notions of causation, the external world, and even the self. Such sweeping skepticism leads to distrust of all broad historical claims.

Should a traveler, returning from a far country, bring us an account of men wholly different from any with whom we were ever acquainted; men, who were entirely divested of avarice, ambition, or revenge; who knew no pleasure but friendship, generosity, and public spirit; we should immediately, from these circumstances, detect the falsehood, and prove him a liar, with the same certainty as if he had stuffed his narration with stories of centaurs and dragons, miracles and prodigies. And if we would explode any forgery in history, we cannot make use of a more convincing argument, than to prove, that the actions ascribed to any person are directly contrary to the course of nature, and that no human motives, in such circumstances, could ever induce him to such a conduct.[38]

Ralph Waldo Emerson (1803-1882), American writer/philosopher in his *Nature* (1836) wrote, "All history becomes subjective; in other words there is properly no history, only biography."

Benjamin Disraeli, 19th Century novelist/British prime minister (1868, 1874-80) wrote this, *"Read no history; nothing but biography, for that is life without theory."*

German philosopher **Friedrich Nietzsche** (1844-1900), *Untimely Meditations, Thus Spake Zarathustra*, spoke of history as "eternal recurrence," because it was propagated as "monumental history." He wrote,

> As long as the soul of historiography is found in the great incentives a powerful man receives from it, as long as the past must be described as something worthy of imitation and is possible a second time, so long, at least, is the past in danger of being somewhat distorted, of being reinterpreted according to aesthetic criteria and so brought closer to fiction.[39]

The **Existentialist Philosophers** in rejecting the enlightenment project and its notions of abstract and absolute truth rejected the possibility of any objectively rational epistemology at all. Christian existentialist philosopher, **Sören Kierkegaard** (1813-1855), *Either/Or*, rightly saw that Hegel's confidence that, unaided by revelation, he could understand the Essence of all history was sheer bombast. However, in providing the existential answer for history, he went from one false solution to another. Fortunately, Kierkegaard found in his personal *Existenz* the saving Christ, but **Heidegger**, **Sartre**, **Jaspers**, et al, found only Angst and estrangement. Having cut themselves off from the possibility of an objective ladder out of the quicksand of subjectivity, and to meaninglessness and ethical (and historical) relativism.

While some would respect the historian, they did not trust the process of history. Playwright **Oscar Wilde** (1854-1900) commented, *"Anybody can make history. Only a great* *man can write it."* **Ambrose Bierce** (1842-1914?), an American satirist, wrote this in his *The Devil's Dictionary* (1906):

> *"HISTORY, n. An account mostly false, of events mostly unimportant, which are brought attention by rulers mostly knaves, and soldiers mostly fools."*

The French philosopher **Jacques Derrida** (1930-2004) coined the word "**deconstruction**" in the 1960s. It is used in contemporary humanities and social sciences to denote a philosophy of meaning that deals with the *ways* that meaning is constructed and understood by writers, texts, and readers. One way of understanding the term is that it involves discovering, recognizing, and understanding the underlying — and unspoken and implicit — assumptions, ideas, and frameworks that form the basis for thought and belief. According to deconstructive readers, one of the "phallogocentrisms" of modernism is the distinction between speech(*logos*) and writing, with writing historically being thought of as derivative to *logos*. In a sense, deconstruction is simply a way to read text (as broadly defined); any deconstruction has a text as its object and subject. This accounts for deconstruction's broad cross-disciplinary scope. Deconstruction has been applied to literature, art, architecture, science, mathematics, philosophy, and psychology, and any other disciplines that can be thought of as involving the act of "marking." One typical form of deconstructive reading is the critique of binary oppositions, or the criticism of dichotomous thought. A central deconstructive argument holds that, in all the classic dualities of Western thought, one term is privileged or "central" over the other. The privileged, central term is the one most associated with the phallus and the *logos*.

Examples include:

- speech over writing
- presence over absence
- identity over difference
- fullness over emptiness
- meaning over meaninglessness
- mastery over submission
- life over death

The implications for historical writing are less apparent than the purely literary. Yet, by applying psycho-sexual words and phrases such as "phallogocentrism," "marking," and the phallus vs. logos," "deconstructionalism" represents a threat to historicism. An obvious derogative is aimed at any attempt to interpret the text outside of the text.

Industrialist **Henry Ford** (1863-1947), first mass-producer of the automobile, once said that *"History is more or less bunk. It's tradition. We don't want tradition. We want to live in the present and the only history that is worth a tinker's damn is the history we make today."* French poet, **Paul Valery** (1871-1945) "Le Cimitiere Marin," wrote *"History is the science of what never happens twice."*

George Santayana (1863-1952), Spanish-American philosopher primarily known for his theories of aesthetics, morality and the spiritual life, uttered the single most quoted statement regarding history: *"Those who cannot remember the past are condemned to repeat it."* Hegel had remarked in his *Philosophy of History* that *"What history and experience teach us is this: that people and government never have learned anything from history or acted on principles deduced from it."* **Winston Churchill** (1871-1947) would transform this into "*The one thing we have learned from history is that we don't learn from history.*"

George Bernard Shaw (1856-1950), Irish author and Fabian Society socialist, added this thought, "*If history repeats itself, and the unexpected always happens, how incapable must man be of learning from experience.*" **Kurt Vonnegut** (1922-2007), American novelist, *Slaughter House Five*, said, "*History is merely a list of surprises. It can only prepare us to be surprised yet again.*"

The modern "phenomenology" of the German philosopher **Edmund Husserl** (1859-1938), brought an approach to philosophy that takes the intuitive experience of phenomena (what presents itself to us in conscious experience) as its starting point and tries to extract from it the essential features of experiences and the essence of what we experience. **Karl Popper** (1902- 1994) is counted among the most influential philosophers of science of the 20th century. He is best known for repudiating the classical observationalist-inductivist account of scientific method by advancing *empirical* falsifiability as the criterion for distinguishing scientific theory from non-science. He is also known for applying critical rationalism, *nomological* explanations of natural science, to history. The ***deductive-nomological***, or **D-N** model is a formalization of scientific explanations in natural language, **Ernest Nagel** (1901-1985) was among the most important philosophers of science in his time. His masterpiece, *The Structure of Science*, published in 1961, practically inaugurated the field of analytic philosophy of science. He invented the idea that, by stating analytic equivalencies (or "bridge laws") between the terms of different sciences, one reduced *ontological* commitment to the entities postulated by the more basic science. Alongside **Rudolf Carnap, Hans Reichenbach, and Carl Hempel**, he remains one of the most enduring figures of the *logical* *positivist* school. Nagel also served as an editor of the *Journal of Philosophy* (1939-1956) and of the *Journal of Symbolic Logic* (1940-1946). Interdisciplinary scholar **Michael Scriven** (fl. 1950-1970), in his *Causes, Connections, and Conditions in History*, has shown that <u>even if we cannot relate causes and effects to each other as formal *nomological* statements, we can often know what caused something</u> (both in history and in disciplines like historical geology). This school of critical rationalism brought implications for *historiography* which are now standard faire.

POSTMODERNISM is a term describing a major movement of intellectual thought which has made a major impact on <u>philosophy</u>, <u>art</u>, <u>critical theory</u>, <u>literature</u>, <u>architecture</u>, <u>history</u>, and <u>culture</u>, especially since the mid <u>20th century</u>. The term has represented many different ideas, but nevertheless, most definitions relate the following:

- A "<u>counter-enlightenment</u>" reaction to *Modernism* – the emphasis of grand, absolute <u>values</u> and establishments
- The belief that no communication is devoid of myth, metaphor, cultural bias and political content (*cultural relativism*)
- Feelings regarding the illegitimacy of <u>knowledge</u> and <u>identity</u> (*nihilism*)
- Asserting that <u>experience is personal (cannot be generalized)</u> and that <u>meaning</u> is only for the individual to experience, not for an author to dictate
- <u>Parody</u>, <u>satire</u>, <u>self-reference</u>, <u>wit</u>
- A culturally <u>pluralistic</u> and profoundly interconnected <u>global society</u> lacking any single dominant center of

political power, communication, or intellectual production.

- A result of a <u>mass media</u> dominated society in which <u>there are only inter-referential</u> representations with <u>no real original referent</u>

The influence of **Modern Literary Theory** can be seen in the landmark appearance of **Hayden White**'s *Metahistory* (1973), and in *The Content of Form: Narrative Discourse and Historical Representation* (1987). White would read the great texts of the 19th Century as if they were novels. This was an attempt to subsume the historiographical enterprise under the canons of literature. The details of what he did are less important than the fact that he did it at all, but this, roughly is what he did. <u>The historian, he argued, has to represent to himself the story of the events</u> contained in the relevant documents. These events he has to 'prefigure' to himself as one of the four main literary tropes of *Metaphor, Metonymy, Synecdoche and Irony*. To these there correspond four literary modes of 'employment' – Romance, Comedy, Tragedy and Satire. The whole schema was based on that put forward by the Canadian literary critic, **Northrop Frye**, in his *Anatomy of Criticism* (1957). **Frank Ankersmit,** (ed) A New Philosophy of History (1995), *History and Tropology: The Rise and Fall of Metaphor* (1990), *Sublime Historical Experience* (2005), examines such issues as the difference between historical representation and artistic expression, the status of metaphor in historical description, and the relation of postmodernism to historicism. Ankersmit's notion of the "sublime historical experience" complicates and challenges existing conceptions of language, truth, and knowledge. The experience unites feelings of loss/pain with those of love/satisfaction, and thus is in agreement with how sublime experience is ordinarily defined. <u>The experience is</u>

precognitive since it precedes (the possibility of) historical knowledge. It compels us to disconnect the notions of experience and truth. As such it is a challenge to traditional conceptions of the relationship between experience and truth or language. Here it would be good to repeat a reference given in Chapter 1:

> The story of modernity and its demise into post-modernity reminds one of the story of the Tower of Babel, related in Genesis 11.... The tower built by modernity has human autonomy as its foundation. The first floor is science, which gives understanding. The second floor is technology, which gives power. The third floor is economics, which gives purpose for scientific and industrial progress. The fourth floor is consumerism, feeding superficial pleasures and driving the economy. This modernist tower, with its pretensions of reaching into heaven, is, like its pagan predecessor, undermined by a confusion of language. This time, however, no divine intervention is needed. Post-modern man himself blows up his own tower by emptying his language of any meaningful content. As Nietzsche had foreseen, the death of God inevitably entailed the death of truth. When man limits himself to unaided human reason, his search for truth must eventually undermine itself. Critical human reason, applied to itself, destroys the very possibility of finding truth. Consequently, ambitious modern man, instead of attaining god-like knowledge and wisdom, ends up with only the frustration of a hopeless quest.[40]

On the whole, questions in the philosophy of history continued to center around fact and explanation, in short, epistemology. The postmodern search for "sufficient cause" can be seen in reaction to the near nihilistic tendencies of many. **R.G. Collingwood** (1889-1943), *The Idea of History* (1936), wrote this:

> *Discovering history's "inner events" via "a priori imagination," proposed that a <u>necessary cause</u> in historical investigation is one such that without it the subsequent actions would make no sense. A <u>sufficient cause</u> is one that would make the course of events that followed considered "rationally required.*[41]

Russian-American sociologist, **Pitirim Sorokin** (1889-1968), wrote in *Social & Cultural Dynamics*,

> *"<u>Intuition, inspiration, revelation</u>... any careful investigator of the history of human experience, science, philosophy, religion and truly creative cultural value, can hardly deny the existence of such <u>a source of truth</u>.* [42]

A general concern is that with "postmodernism" we have lost our historical bearings. The theological and metaphysical bases of our culture have disintegrated. **Keith Jenkins**, *Rethinking History* (1991), attacked approaches to history which suggested that most writing about the past is nothing more than a literary construct, that <u>history was an aesthetic/literary genre such that it could not be an epistemology and that, therefore, the questions historians normally considered,</u> the relationship of facts to values, of interpretation, of objectivity, truth, etc., <u>were incapable of being answered.</u> Jenkins thought that <u>debates about 'history' are debates about meaning (i.e. *ontological* debates) and, of course, meaning (of the 'facts'; of this or that interpretation).</u> He asserted that <u>all historical discourse is positioned, is ideological/political</u>, and that, rather than avoid this obvious conclusion, one should make explicit one's own position... that is to say, there was a call for 'reflexivity' going 'all the way down.

Conflict within Christianity and the "secular humanist" battle is revealed in the writings of many.

Pierre Teilhard de Chardin (1881-1955), a Jesuit priest trained as a paleontologist and philosopher, and who was present at the discovery of Peking Man, abandoned the literal interpretation of the creation account in Genesis in favor of a metaphorical interpretation. He named this approach "Mystical Naturalism."

In reaction to Herman Dooyeweerd, Edward John Carnell and Cornelius Van Til, **Francis Schaeffer** (1912-1984), *How Shall We Then Live*, opposed such theological modernism. He promoted an orthodox protestant faith and a "*presuppositional*" approach to Christian apologetics. In the defense of our Christian faith, we first simply proclaim the gospel, clearing up any misunderstandings, and responding to the objections of unbelief. Secondly, apologetics addresses the willful suppression of ones knowledge of God, worldly wisdom for the folly it is. The aim is to show that the Christian worldview gives a coherent explanation of man and his experiences, whereas the unbeliever's worldview makes nonsense out of history, science and even reasoning itself.

Here, we simply are asking the question, "Have the various non-Christian worldviews we have unwittingly or purposefully adopted compromised our ability to both present the gospel and to address faulty worldviews?" Why do we so easily concede faulty assumptions "for the sake of argument," for example. Has anyone ever been argued into believing the claims of Jesus?

Who is the One that will convince the unbeliever? Is it my testimony proclaimed more loudly than his? Is it the logic of the choice? Divine revelation through the work of the Holy Spirit must have some part in the activity. Over this the apologist has no control except by intercession with God. The truth from this point of view is that the unbeliever is committed to materialism, not by deep conviction, but by fear of the alternative,

> *particularly biblical theism. Thus, at bottom, at least some naturalists own up to being driven by a deeply entrenched desire to avoid God, even if that commits them to an irrational, self-refuting worldview.* [43]

CHAPTER 5
HISTORY AS METAPHOR

An intriguing concept for meta-history is that of "meaning." Does this piece of history we now examine have meaning? "Meaning" is a concept that has significance only for humans. With it we leave all the natural sciences, for by common consent they have no place for this concept. Of course, the laws of nature and the problems of *cosmology* have meaning for the scientists who work on them, but meaning is not one of the phenomena they work on.[44]

Meaning is a slippery concept. It can relate either to significance or to symbolism. In one sense we can say of an event that it is full of meaning (or meaningful) because it is perceived as significant. In another, and most common in philosophy, it connects with words or other symbols. This is the realm of semantics. The basic philosophical problem of meaning is that of how words relate to the world. What is clear for our purposes is that the ability to see the significance of some event or cultural construct (a ritual, for example), and the ability to understand a word, a sentence, a page or a book are all exclusively human attributes.[45]

It may be argued that "meaning" is distinctly divine and that only mankind, made in the image of God, can grasp such meaning. He does so through his God-given ability to communicate with others, through language, through social intercourse. Language in this sense is much more than "symbol A = meaning B." It is based on the assumption that we can communicate at all, that we can share our values and sense of worth or purpose. It is no less meaningful to understand history than it is to know the God of history.

We often see the complexity of history in terms of something simpler that we can understand. History is more than a summary of chronological fact. It is characterized by selection of representative facts, implications and generalizations. No history text or news story is written without bias or worldview affecting the process of presentation.

> *"Most people need some degree of simplification. This can often be done by analogy — a comparison with something simpler and more familiar. Yet analogies can always be dangerous — never more so than when ideas are drawn from one area and unquestioningly applied to another.... These patterns of history present themselves from an arrangement of elements or units which through repetition, become identifiable and recognizable."* [46]

Although philosophers of history do not generally present historical approaches as analogy, I do so here for the sake of discussion of *worldview*:

1) History as **DRAMA** - Everybody loves a good story.

> *"A certain man went down from Jerusalem to Jericho, and fell among thieves who stripped him of his clothing, wounded him and departed..."* (Luke 10:30-37)

History is an anthology of heroes and villains who prove themselves worthy actors on the stage of life and who invoke readable and enjoyable narrative.

Danger: The attempt to see history as a wholly linguistic activity lies in the contrast with purely historical activity. Literary activity is self-refcrential; "A poem should not mean, but be" (Archibald McLeish, "Ars Poetica"). History refers to objects outside or beyond itself.

2) History as **REPETITION** - Nothing ever really changes.

   "That which has been is what will be, That which is done is what will be done, And there is nothing new under the sun."(Eccles 1:9)

Human nature and natural law create cyclic repetition, rise and fall.

Danger: Nice theory! Where's the evidence? Change may be the single most consistent characteristic of history, predictable change rather rare.

3) History as **EVOLUTION** - Things are getting better.

   "But we all... are being transformed into the same image from glory to glory..."(2 Cor 3:17) "But one thing I do, forgetting those things which are behind and reaching forward to those things which are ahead, I press toward the goal for the prize of the upward call of God in Christ Jesus." (Phil 3:13-14)

History is a record of progress toward perfection.

Danger: This theory lacks attraction during tough times. It especially flies in the face of the biblical depiction of the "last days" which will bring great misery and folly.

4) History as **STRUGGLE** - Somebody is trying to take your stuff away.

"Man who is born of woman is of few days and full of trouble."(Job 14:1)

There is an inevitable struggle between classes and control of production.

Danger: Struggle is absent both in absolute tyranny and when people are free and prosperous.

5) History as **SCIENCE** - We are getting smarter and more careful.

"[The Bereans] were more fair-minded... in that they received the word with all readiness, and searched the Scriptures daily to find out whether these things were so."(Acts 17:11)

We can know only what we can experience and rigorously measure.

Danger: Humans possess a distinct capability unlike all other animals, that of logic, creative explanation and wise prediction, sometimes without apparent experiential referent.

6) History as **PROPAGANDA** - Everything is seen from somebody's bias.

"Beware of the scribes, who desire to go around in long robes, love greetings in the marketplaces, the best seats in

the synagogues, and the best places at feasts, who devour widows' houses, and for a pretense make long prayers. These will receive greater condemnation. (Mark 12:38–40)

Historical methods and presuppositions tend to be regional, subjective and selective.

Danger: There is divine overview and supervision. There are measures for bias and motivation for accuracy and truthfulness.

7) History as **RANDOM OCCURRENCE** - Things just happen.

"Vanity, vanity, all is vanity"(Eccles 1:2) "What is man that Thou art mindful of him" (Psa 8:4)"

All we like sheep have gone astray..., everyone to his own way."(Psa 53:6)

"Come now you who say 'we shall go'... You do not know what your life will be like tomorrow. You are just a vapor that appears for a little while and then vanishes away."(James 4:13-14)

We cannot speculate beyond a random occurrence of discontinuous interruptions without purpose.

Danger: The Bible urges us to learn from others, to heed warning and to trust promise and prophecy.

8) History as **GOD'S PROVIDENCE** - God planned it this way.

"To everything there is a season and a purpose under heaven."(Eccles 3:1)

"[Christ] is the firstborn over all creation... and in Him all things consist."(Col 1:16-17)

History is a Theocentric *Eschatology* with purpose, design and providential sovereignty.

Danger: Sovereignty does not mean the absence of free will; God names the terms of His sovereignty, not Calvin, nor Funk & Wagnalls for that matter.

CHAPTER 6
THE CHRISTIAN MANDATE

In Scripture, God admonished His children to learn from history.[47] "Remember the days of old; consider the years of many generations" (Deut 32:7). "Give ear, O my people, to my teaching; incline your ears to the words of my mouth! I will open my mouth in a parable; I will utter dark sayings from of old, things that we have heard and known, that our fathers have told us. We will not hide them from their children, but tell to the coming generation..." (Psa 78:1-3). God's Word repeatedly rehearses Israel's history (Deut Chapters 1-3; Josh 24:1-13; Psa 105, 106 and 136). Even in the New Testament, the apostle Paul reviewed some Old Testament history (1 Cor 10:1-10). He then explained one reason to study such history: "Now these things happened to them as an example, but they were written down for our instruction." In Acts 7, Stephen delivered a long history lecture before his hearers stoned him to death.

Why did God include so many history lessons (conscious reflections about the past) as well as basic history (accounts of what happened) in His inerrant Word? Biblical history helped reinforce the special identity of God's people, but more importantly, it reminded them of His faithfulness. He had worked with a mighty arm in the past. That would reassure them that, despite occasional chastening, He would keep His covenants and fulfill His promises for the present and future. Believers today are blessed by reading this history too.

Of course, God did not retire from involvement in the unfolding of history after biblical times. He did not cease acting in human history after the closing of the Canon. Christians should study God's working in His church through the ages. They should be fully aware of the historical unfolding of biblical prophecy which continues after the time of Jesus up through His return. This is the study of biblical eschatology. Other compelling reasons for Christians to study history include faith enhancement, enjoyment, gaining wisdom, citizenship training, and identity development. History, as a field of study, deserves a high status in the church of Jesus Christ.

PART III
WORLD RELIGIONS & CHRISTIAN EXCEPTIONALITY

CHAPTER 7
WHY STUDY WORLD RELIGIONS?

... you will seek the LORD your God, and you will find Him if you seek Him with all your heart and with all your soul (Deut 4:29).

One of our members brought his atheist friend who was in a doctorate program. He sat across the table from us. He introduced himself as a "non-theist." Perhaps he thought that more palatable to a group of Christians. He said that Christians are just another religion with their own book, one like all the others with non-provable assertions of a god, of salvation and after-life. His blithe disregard for our well-thought out faith upset some, raised questions which we were anxious to ask of him and, admittedly, left others of us dumbfounded. It was a Christian philosophy group which called itself "Mars Hill" after Paul's reasoned evangelism in Athens described in the book of Acts. We had boasted that all were welcome to participate in attendance and discussion. Of course, such openness presumes a strong group leader with a strong faith and a knowledge of others' beliefs.

But sanctify the Lord God in your hearts, and always be ready to give a defense to everyone who asks you a reason for the hope that is in you, with meekness and fear (1 Pet 3:15).

We were ill-prepared to talk to him. That experience taught me that reason alone cannot persuade a non-believer to cross the threshold of faith into Christian experience. Reason must follow faith. This is proof enough for me that it does no good for any of us to be a "Jesus salesman." It is the Spirit of God which brings conviction upon each heart of its great need to believe and to trust Jesus.

Then, why study world religions? Ronald Knox once quipped that "the study of comparative religions is the best way to become comparatively religious". This is not a flattering comment on the fruits of curiosity. It points to the first difference in Christianity from all religions. The first tenant of Christian faith is not that we sought God, but that He sought us (Gal 4:4; John 3:16-17). He loved us before we knew Him. And He brings a salvation which we cannot earn. If it were merely a matter of studying what each and all of the religions of the world had to offer and then choosing the best one, this study would be invaluable to ones' salvation. But that is not the way it works at all.

For the time will come when they will not endure sound doctrine, but according to their own desires, because they have itching ears, they will heap up for themselves teachers (2 Tim 4:3).

Regardless of what we want to hear, *"there is a need for salvation that has been imprinted on the human soul since the first couple went astray in the Garden. The desire is universal, and every religion and worldview offers some form of redemption. For the Buddhist, it is nirvana; for the Jew, it is the atonement of good works; for the Muslim, it may be heaven after a perilous walk across the sword of judgment. But religions and philosophies are not the only ones offering redemption. Any belief system in the marketplace of ideas, any movement that attracts followers, anything that has the power to grab people's hearts and win their allegiance does so because it taps into the deepest longings. And those longings are, ultimately, religious. Just as every worldview offers an answer to the question of how we got here (creation), and an analysis of the basic human dilemma (the Fall), so every worldview offers a way to solve that dilemma (redemption). But which offer of redemption is true? Which gives a genuine answer to the human dilemma? And which ones are crass counterfeits?* [48]

It is probably correct to say that the pool of religious beliefs and teachings is an insoluble morass of confusion and contradiction. A life-time of study and strain would yield little more than a pessimistic view of religion itself rather than a "best choice" by reason and analysis alone. Why then study world religions at all? There is certainly not a Biblical imperative to do so. But if a Christian is motivated

- to obey the Great Commission of Matthew 28 to go into all the world and preach the gospel,

it would benefit the missionary to know how his potential converts think and behave. Jesus had that advantage with the Woman at the Well. Paul had that advantage in Athens because of his familiarity with Greek culture. The writer of Hebrews had that advantage in preaching to the newly converted Jew. "I am all things to all people that I might by any means save some," Paul would say. It is beneficial for us in America to know how the secular humanist thinks, let alone to know what is going on with a Zoroastrian or Zen Buddhist.

> For though I am free from all men, I have made myself a servant to all, that I might win the more; and to the Jews I became as a Jew, that I might win Jews; to those who are under the law, as under the law, that I might win those who are under the law; to those who are without law, as without law (not being without law toward God, but under law toward Christ), that I might win those who are without law; to the weak I became as weak, that I might win the weak. I have become all things to all men, that I might by all means save some. Now this I do for the gospel's sake, that I may be partaker of it with you (1 Cor 9:19-23).

Yet, we should ponder why earlier in the same epistle Paul expressed this:

> For I determined not to know anything among you except Jesus Christ and Him crucified. I was with you in weakness, in fear, and in much trembling. And my speech and my preaching were not with persuasive words of human wisdom, but in demonstration of the Spirit and of power, that your faith should not be in the wisdom of men but in the power of God (1 Cor 2:2-5).

We do not study others' background and religious presumptions in order to argue from their point of view, but rather, to discover a starting place from which to explain the gospel simply and in concert with the Holy Spirit Who has none of our limitations of language or human understanding. The Bible instructs us not to worry about what we will say in defense of the faith, because <u>He will give us the words</u> when the time comes.

> *But when they arrest you and deliver you up, do not worry beforehand, or premeditate what you will speak. But whatever is given you in that hour, speak that; for it is not you who speak, but the Holy Spirit* (Mark 13:11).

- Another reason to study world religions and belief systems is <u>to recognize, to debunk and then to counteract their influence.</u>

> *Now the Spirit expressly says that in latter times some will depart from the faith, giving heed to deceiving spirits and doctrines of demons, speaking lies in hypocrisy, having their own conscience seared with a hot iron, forbidding to marry, and commanding to abstain from foods which God created to be received with thanksgiving by those who believe and know the truth. For every creature of God is good, and nothing is to be refused if it is received with thanksgiving; for it is sanctified by the word of God and prayer. If you instruct the brethren in these things, you will be a good minister of Jesus Christ, nourished in the words of faith and of the good doctrine which you have carefully followed* (1 Tim 4:1-6).

At first blush some of these religions seem to be almost Christian. So, before one studies world religions one should read and know the Christian Bible. Only then will he immediately recognize the differences. Moreover, one should know the Savior personally and have a walking talking relationship with the Holy Spirit Who will guide him through the confusion. The Bible warns the believer to have nothing to do with the occult, to expel the apostate and to "<u>try the spirits whether they are of God, because many false prophets are gone out into the world</u>"

> *Beloved, do not believe every spirit, but test the spirits, whether they are of God; because many false prophets have gone out into the world. By this you know the Spirit of God: Every spirit that confesses that Jesus Christ has come in the flesh is of God, and every spirit that does not confess that Jesus Christ has come in the flesh is not of God. And this is the spirit of the Antichrist, which you have heard was coming, and is now already in the world. You are of God, little children, and have overcome them, because He who is in you is greater than he who is in the world. They are of the world. Therefore they speak as of the world, and the world hears them. We are of God. He who knows God hears us; he who is not of God does not hear us. By this we know the spirit of truth and the spirit of error* (1 John 4:1-6).

- A third reason for the Christian study of comparative religions is to appreciate the uniqueness of Christianity.

It is in several ways not like other religions. Some claim that it is not a religion at all. Remember our provisional definition: **Religion is the effort to live harmoniously with the power or powers one believes are controlling the world.** But that doesn't seem to define Christianity satisfactorily. Living harmoniously with God is important, but the Christian isn't interested in living harmoniously with the devil who has certain dominion in this world. <u>There is no</u>

definition of religion into which Christianity will fit except its own biblically defined doctrine. It is at odds with all religions and shares no foundational similarity with any of them. It may be useful, then, to talk briefly of several major world religions and to contrast Christianity with each of them to prove the point.

There are about seven billion people in the world most of which are associated with one or another of the world's major religions. 2.4 billion are Christian, 1.6 billion Islam, 1 billion Hindu and 376 million Buddhist. Not only do most people have little knowledge of the world's major religions but are woefully shallow in understanding their own religion. A common misconception is that all religions are basically the same and represent different paths to the same God. Years ago a retired military chaplain ministered in our church. He had spent a good deal of time in Saudi Arabia and reminded us that we share a belief with the Muslims in the God of Abraham. What he failed to point out is that the Muslim does not personally know the God of Abraham. The beliefs of Islam do not parallel that of Judaism or Christianity. Although similar teachings occur in various religions, in truth the study of these religions proves that there are greater differences than there are similarities. Montgomery has said that "the characteristic most fully shared by the religions of the world is their incompatibility with each other."[49]

CHAPTER 8
AN OVERVIEW OF RELIGION

Regional and Historic Origin

Religious traditions fall into super-groups in comparative religion, arranged by historical origin and mutual influence. Abrahamic religions originate in the Middle East, Indian religions in the Indian subcontinent and East Asian religions in East Asia. Another group with supra-regional influence are Afro-American religions, which have their origins in Central and West Africa.

- Abrahamic religions are the largest group, and these consist mainly of Christianity, Islam, Judaism and the Bahá'í Faith. They are named for the patriarch Abraham, and are unified by the practice of monotheism. Today, around 3.4 billion people are followers of Abrahamic religions and are spread widely around the world apart from the regions around Southeast Asia. Several Abrahamic organizations are vigorous proselytizers.

- Indian religions originated in Greater India and tend to share a number of key concepts, such as dharma and karma. They are of the most influence across the Indian subcontinent, East Asia, Southeast Asia, as well as isolated parts of Russia. The main Indian religions are Hinduism, Jainism, Buddhism and Sikhism.

- The East Asian religions make use of the concept of *Tao* (in Chinese) or *Dō* (in Japanese or Korean), namely Taoism and Confucianism, both of which are asserted by some scholars to be non-religious in nature. But, in fact, they are very much religious, just not theistic.

- Indigenous ethnic religions, formerly found on every continent, now are marginalized by the major organized faiths, but persisting as undercurrents of folk religion. This includes traditional African religions, Asian Shamanism, Native American religions, Austronesian and Australian Aboriginal traditions, Chinese folk religion, and postwar Shintoism. Under more traditional listings, this has been referred to as "paganism" along with historical polytheism.

- Iranian religions originated in Iran and include Zoroastrianism, Yazdânism, Ahl-e Haqq and historical traditions of Gnosticism (Mandaeism,Manichaeism). It has significant overlaps with Abrahamic traditions, e.g. in Sufism and in recent movements such as Bábism and the Bahá'í Faith.

- "New religious" or "new age" movement is the term applied to any religious faith which has emerged since the 19th century, often syncretizing, re-interpreting or reviving aspects of older traditions: Hindu reform movements, Eckankar, Ayyavazhi, polytheistic reconstructionism, and so forth.

View of God - One of the sharp lines of demarcation is a religion's view of god. These generally fall into the following classifications:

- Monotheistic - The doctrine or belief that there is only one god.

Hear, O Israel: The LORD our God, the LORD is one! (Deut 6:4)

- Polytheistic - The worship of or belief in more than one god.

Do not go after other gods to serve them and worship them, and do not provoke Me to anger with the works of your hands; and I will not harm you (Jer 25:6).

- Pantheistic - A doctrine identifying the deity with the universe and its phenomena such that god and nature are the same thing; god is everything and everything is god. The Bible presents God as holy, sovereign, omnipresent, omniscient, omnipotent, self-existent, eternal, immutable, perfect and infinite. None of these are compatible with pantheism. God transcends all of his creation.

  Professing to be wise, they became fools, and changed the glory of the incorruptible God into an image made like corruptible man and birds and four-footed animals and creeping things (Rom 1:22-23).

- Atheistic - Disbelief in or denial that there is a god or gods

  The fool has said in his heart, "There is no God." They are corrupt, They have done abominable works, There is none who does good. The LORD looks down from heaven upon the children of men, To see if there are any who understand, who seek God. They have all turned aside, They have together become corrupt; There is none who does good, No, not one (Psalm 14:1-3).

Since the late 19th century, the demographics of religion have changed a great deal. Some countries with a historically large Christian population have experienced a significant decline in the numbers of professed active Christians. Symptoms of the decline in active participation in Christian religious life include declining recruitment for the priesthood and monastic life, as well as diminishing attendance at church. On the other hand, since the 19th century, large areas of Sub-Saharan Africa have been converted to Christianity, and this area of the world has the highest population growth rate. In the realm of Western culture, there has been an increase in the number of people who identify themselves as secular humanists. In many countries, such as the People's Republic of China, communist governments have discouraged religion, making it difficult to count the actual number of believers. However, after the collapse of communism in numerous countries of Eastern Europe and the former Soviet Union, religious life has been experiencing resurgence there, both in the form of traditional Eastern Christianity and particularly in the forms of Neo-paganism and East Asian religions.

CHAPTER 9
A BRIEF DESCRIPTION OF THE MAJOR RELIGIONS
AND THEIR CONTRAST WITH CHRISTIANITY

Worldwide, more than eight-in-ten people identify with a religious group. A comprehensive demographic study of more than 230 countries and territories conducted by the Pew Research Center's Forum on Religion & Public Life estimates that there are 5.8 billion religiously affiliated adults and children around the globe, representing 84% of the 2010 world population of 6.9 billion. This demographic study – based on an analysis of more than 2,500 censuses, surveys and population registers yields the following data:

Size of Major Religious Groups, 2016, by Starfunker226 (Own work) CC-BY-SA-3.0 via Wikimedia Commons **Percentage of the global population:**

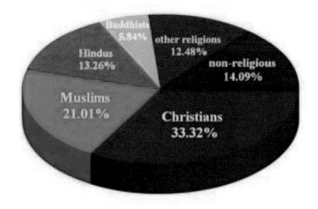

World Religions by percentage

Other religions include followers of African traditional religions, Chinese folk religions, Native american religions and Australian aboriginal religions, Bahai's, Jains, Sikhs, Shintoists, Taoists, followers of Tennikyo, Wiccans, Zoroastrians and many other faiths. Percentages may not add to 100 due to rounding

A 2012 Pew study reveals the following demographic:

Christians	31.5%	2.2 billion
Muslims	23.2%	1.6 billion
Unaffiliated	16.3%	1.1 billion
Hindus	15.0%	1.0 billion
Buddhists	7.1%	500 million
Folk Religions	5.9%	400 million
Other Religions	0.8%	58 million
Jews	0.2%	14 million

Folk Religions include African traditional religions, Chinese folk religions, Native American religions and Australian aboriginal religions. Other Religions include Baha'i faith, Jainism, Sikhism, Shintoism, Taoism, Tenrikyo, Wicca and Zoroastrianism, to mention just a few. It is instructive to realize that three-quarters of the religiously unaffiliated live in the massive and populous Asia-Pacific region. 700 million alone are in China. It is encouraging to know that Christianity is the most evenly dispersed across the world's geography. Darker shading represents a greater prevalence of the majority religion:

The largest religious groups worldwide

Largest religions by country in 2010 (darker colour represents greater prevalence)

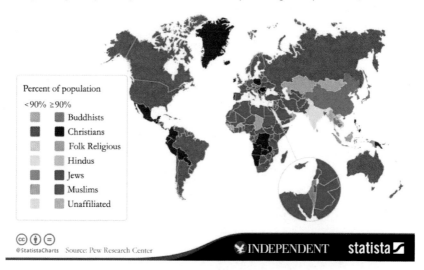

Percent of population

<90% ≥90%

- Buddhists
- Christians
- Folk Religious
- Hindus
- Jews
- Muslims
- Unaffiliated

@StatistaCharts   Source: Pew Research Center

✿INDEPENDENT   statista

The Ka'aba is a cuboid-shaped building in Mecca, Saudi Arabia, and is the most sacred site in Islam. The building has a mosque built around it, the Masjid al-Haram. All Muslims around the world are supposed to face the Ka'aba during prayers no matter where they are in the world.

Islam emanates from its prophet Mohammed in the seventh century A.D. It is monotheistic and characterized by a submission to its god Allah and prophet Mohammed, who is considered to be the chief and last prophet of God. Muslims believe that God is one and incomparable, that the purpose of existence is to love and serve God. Muslims also believe that Islam is the complete and universal version of a primordial faith that was revealed at many times and places before, including through Abraham, Moses and Jesus, whom they consider prophets. They maintain that previous messages and revelations have been partially changed or corrupted over time, but consider the Qur'an to be both the unaltered and the final revelation of God. Religious concepts and practices include the five pillars of Islam, which are basic concepts and obligatory acts of worship, and following Islamic law, which touches on virtually every aspect of life and society, providing guidance on a variety of topics from banking and welfare, to warfare and the environment.

The 'Five Pillars' of Islam are the foundation of Muslim life:

- Faith or belief in the Oneness of God and the finality of the prophethood of Muhammad;
- Establishment of the daily prayers;
- Concern for and almsgiving to the needy;
- Self-purification through fasting; and
- The pilgrimage to Mecca for those who are able.

Some call *jihad* the "sixth pillar of Islam." Broadly, jihad is "the struggle in the way of god" or "the fight in the way of Allah." One Qur'anic passage commands Muslims to "fight against those who do not believe in Allah or the judgment day (9:29).

75-90% of Muslims are <u>Sunni</u>. Sunni is the branch of Islam that accepts the first four caliphs as rightful successors of Mohammed. The second largest sect, <u>Shia</u>, makes up 10–20% and believe that following the Prophet Muhammad's death, leadership should have passed directly to his cousin/son-in-law, <u>Ali bin Abu Talib</u>. The most populous Muslim-majority country is Indonesia, home to 12.7% of the world's Muslims followed by Pakistan (11.0%), Bangladesh (9.2%) and <u>Egypt</u> (4.9%). Sizable minorities are also found in <u>India</u>, <u>China</u>, <u>Russia</u>, and parts of <u>Europe</u>. With about 1.6 to 1.7 billion followers or 22 to 24% of <u>earth's population</u>, Islam is the <u>second-largest</u> and the <u>fastest-growing religion in the world</u> due to the fact that of all the major religions it has the lowest median age and the highest birth rate. Muslims make up a majority of the population in 49 countries, the largest of which is Indonesia.

Accepting Jesus as a prophet, though subordinate in importance to Mohammed and Moses, Muslims do not see His person and work in the same light as Christians. <u>They do not believe in the incarnate Son of God nor in His resurrection. These, of course, are cornerstones of the Christian faith</u>.

And the Word became flesh and dwelt among us, and we beheld His glory, the glory as of the only begotten of the Father, full of grace and truth. ...And I have seen and testified that this is the Son of God (John 1:14; 34).

I and My Father are one (John 10:30).

And if Christ is not risen, your faith is futile; you are still in your sins! (Cor 15:17)

Neither do the Muslims consider Jesus as Savior. They believe that equating anyone with God is blasphemy. Hmm, that is exactly what the Jews thought of Jesus! Different also is their view of God. Unlike the God of the Bible, Allah has done nothing for man that cost him anything. Islam makes no real provision for sin. One's salvation is never certain since it is based on a works system and on complete surrender ("Islam") to the will of Allah. This religion rejects the crucifixion and resurrection of Jesus, though it concedes that He was a sinless prophet. Mohammed did not rise from the dead, and there is no basis for resurrection in Islam. The god of Islam is a very capricious one, too far removed from people to be personally involved or concerned. Not only is he impersonal, but he also emphasizes judgment to the exclusion of love, and he motivates people by fear rather than by grace.

Islamic Extremism, or radical Islam, sometimes called Islamic Fundamentalism, is driven by an interpretation of Islam that believes that Islamic, or sharia, law is an all-encompassing system demanded by Allah which must be instituted by a global Islamic state. As such, Islamic extremists consider it to be the only truly legitimate form of governance. Thus, the ultimate objective is the merger of "mosque and state" under sharia law. Those who favor such an approach are called Islamists. Their ideology is called Islamism, or political Islam. In their mind they are promoting justice and freedom by instituting sharia. Acts of Islamic extremism include terrorism, human rights abuses, the advancement of sharia-based governance, bigotry towards non-Muslims and rival Muslims and overall hostility to the West and, in particular, Western democracy. A Muslim is only guaranteed an entrance into heaven when he commits to martyrdom *"fi sabilillah,"* in the cause of

Allah. The philosophy and practice of "gradualism" shows its intent to take over the entire world. All must either convert or die. The largest Islamic extremist group to use the methods of "gradualism" is the Muslim Brotherhood. State sponsors of terrorism include Iran, Syria and Sudan, with the Iranian government being the largest. Iran supports terrorist groups such as Hezbollah, Al-Qaeda, the Taliban, Hamas, Palestinian Islamic Jihad and the Popular Front for the Liberation of Palestine-General Command. Iran also supports radical militias in Iraq and Yemen and directly participates in acts of terrorism globally. But the enemy of Christianity is not so much terrorism as it is Islamic Jihad (holy war against infidels). Under Islam the Qur'an is very clear about what to do to the infidels – cut off their heads, cut off their fingers and toes, smite them on their heads because they disobeyed Allah. Taken literally the Qur'an instructs and encourages Muslims to kill infidels, kill apostates, kill those who do not believe in Allah or have gone against his path. Islamism is a religion of "death," whereas Christianity is a religion of "life." While there is much infighting and inability to organize among the Muslims, there is one cause that can rally them together – hatred of the Jewish state and Western civilization. Islamic fundamentalism is the driving force that is rallying the Muslims to "Jihad" for obliterating Israel and replacing the Western world order. Extremists narrowly define jihad as the struggle against infidels. Dying on behalf of this cause brings promise in the after-life of seventy-two virgins willing to fulfill every fantasy – quite an incentive for young jihadist men. Christianity has no such motivation to kill non-believers nor to commit suicide for the sake of the caliphate (Islamic state). We most certainly believe in "giving our lives for the cause of Christ." But the Bible teaches that Jesus came to bring abundant life.

Hinduism was founded c.1500 B.C. in India and is the third largest religion in the world. With a stable population of about 900 million home shrines and temples provide places of worship. Its leaders are gurus or sages. Its sacred texts are Vedas, Upanishads, Sutras and Bhagavad Gita. Its followers are pantheists with polytheistic elements who consider the ultimate reality to be Brahman, the holy and sacred power that is thought to be the sustainer the universe. Human nature is thought to be in bondage to ignorance and illusion, but able to escape. Purpose in life is to attain liberation from the cycle of reincarnation, where karma unresolved causes

The Swaminarayan sect's Akshardham Temple in Delhi, according the Guinness World Records is the World's Largest Comprehensive Hindu Temple

the soul to be born into a new body; karma resolved achieves moksa (liberation). Karma then is the moral law of cause and effect that determines the direction of rebirth. Hinduism's supreme being is the undefinable essence of the universe, impersonal Brahman, a philosophical absolute.

But, the God of Christianity is loving and keenly interested in the affairs of men, quite in contrast to the aloof deity of Hinduism. The Hindu views man as a manifestation of the impersonal Brahman, without individual self or self-worth. <u>Christianity teaches that man was made in the image of God with a personality and the ability to receive and give love.</u> Wrong-doing to the Hindu is merely an indication of ignorance. <u>Christianity sees sin as a real act of rebellion against a perfect and Holy God</u>.

> *Against You, You only, have I sinned, And done this evil in Your sight - That You may be found just when You speak, And blameless when You judge* (Psalm 51:4).

> *For all have sinned and fall short of the glory of God* (Rom 3:23)

For the Hindu salvation can be attained in the way of knowledge, the way of devotion or the way of works (ceremonial ritual). <u>The Christian's way of salvation is through Jesus Christ, and that alone</u>.

> *For by grace you have been saved through faith, and that not of yourselves; it is the gift of God, not of works, lest anyone should boast* (Eph 2:8-9).

> *But when the kindness and the love of God our Savior toward man appeared, not by works of righteousness which we have done, but according to His mercy He saved us, through the washing of regeneration and renewing of the Holy Spirit, whom He poured out on us abundantly through Jesus Christ our Savior, that having been justified by His grace we should become heirs according to the hope of eternal life* (Titus 3:4-7).

He who believes in the Son has everlasting life; and he who does not believe the Son shall not see life, but the wrath of God abides on him (John 3:36).

Also, Christianity views the world as an entity eternally different in nature and separate from God, not part of some universal or monistic Oneness. The two religions could never be reconciled; they are mutually exclusive.

Sikhism, a monotheistic religion born in northern India in the sixth century A.D., combines elements of both Hinduism and Islam. It is the fifth-largest organized religion in the world, with approximately 24 million Sikhs. This system of religiousphilosophy and expression has been traditionally known as the Gurmat (literally 'wisdom of the Guru'). Punjab, in northwest India is the only region in the world with a majority Sikh population. Sikhs are expected to embody the

qualities of a "Sant-Sipāhī" – a saint-soldier. One must have control over one's internal vices and be able to be constantly immersed in virtues clarified in the Guru Granth Sahib.

A Sikh man at Golden Temple, Amritsar (Harmandir Sahib)

Jainism is an ascetic religion of India founded in the sixth century B.C. It now has about 4.3 million adherents. Although it denies the existence of a supreme being, it teaches the immortality and transmigration of the soul.

It prescribes a path of non-violence towards all living beings. Its philosophy and practice emphasize the necessity of self-effort to move the soul toward divine consciousness and liberation. Any soul that has conquered its own inner enemies and achieved the state of supreme being is called a *jina* ("conqueror" or "victor"). Jainism is a religion of legalism, for one attains his own salvation only through the path of rigid self-denial. There is no freedom in this religion, only rules. In contrast to the

Five Mahavratas of Jain ascetics

The Jain symbol that was agreed upon by all Jain sects in 1974

self-effort of Jainism the salvation of Christianity sets one free through Jesus Christ:

> *Therefore if the Son makes you free, you shall be free indeed* (John 8:36).

> *Come to Me, all you who labor and are heavy laden, and I will give you rest. Take My yoke* upon you and

learn from Me, for I am gentle and lowly in heart, and you will find rest for your souls. For My yoke is easy and My burden is light (Matt 11:28-30).

Buddhism, founded by its name-sake in the fifth century B.C., is based on teachings attributed to <u>Siddhartha Gautama</u>, who is commonly known as the <u>Buddha</u> (meaning "the awakened one"). It teaches that suffering is inseparable from existence but that inward extinction of the self and worldly desire culminates in a state of spiritual enlightenment beyond both suffering and existence. The teachings on the Four Noble Truths are regarded as central to the teachings of Buddhism, and are said to provide a conceptual framework for Buddhist thought. These four

Monks debating at Sera Monastery, Tibet

The *Dharmachakra* repre sents the <u>Noble Eightfold Path</u>.

truths explain the nature of *dukkha* (suffering, anxiety, dissatisfaction), its causes, and how it can be overcome. They can be summarized as follows:

1. The truth of *dukkha* (suffering, anxiety, dissatisfaction)
2. The truth of the origin of *dukkha*
3. The truth of the cessation of *dukkha*
4. The truth of the path leading to the cessation of *dukkha*

The path leading to cessation of *dukkha* includes Right View (or Right Understanding), Right Intention (or Right Thought), Right Speech, Right Action, Right Livelihood, Right Effort, Right Mindfulness, and Right Concentration. There are about 400 million Buddhists in the world.

Zen Buddhism is a form of Buddhism that became popular in China, Korea and Japan and that lays special emphasis on meditation. Zen places less emphasis on scriptures than some other forms of Buddhism and prefers to focus on direct spiritual breakthroughs to truth.

Zen Buddhist teaching is often full of paradox, in order to loosen the grip of the ego and to facilitate the penetration into the realm of the True Self or Formless Self, which is equated with the Buddha himself. According to Zen master Kosho Uchiyama, when thoughts and fixation on the little "I" are transcended, an Awakening to a universal, non-dual Self occurs: "When we let go of thoughts and wake up to the reality of life that is working beyond them, we discover the Self that is living universal non-dual life (before the separation into two) that pervades all living creatures and all existence." Thinking and thought must therefore not be allowed to confine and bind one. Buddhism is a promise that certain meditative practices and mind trainings can effectively show us how to awaken our Buddha-nature and liberate us from suffering and confusion. Nirvana is seen as the release from suffering and rebirth that brings inner peace.

There is a Zen Buddhist statement which says, "The mind of man is like the wind in a pine tree in a Chinese ink drawing." In this, man is killed twice. He is only the wind in the pine tree, and even then only in a drawing. Christianity teaches the very reverse of what the Eastern thinker says. Man can understand and respond to the One who, having made him and communicated with him, called upon him to show that he loved Him by simple command: "Don't do this." The test could have been something else. No act of primitive magic is involved here. This is the infinite-personal God calling on personal man to act by choice. And it was a motivated command, "...for in the day that you eat of it you shall surely die," which would make no sense if man is only a machine. He would so act by choice because he was created to be different from the animal, the plant and the machine.[50]

In Buddhism there is no personal creator, and the world is seen as operating by natural power and law, not divine command. Since there is no personal god, only the Buddha is venerated. <u>There is no reconciliation with or similarity to Christianity</u>.

Confucianism could be called a religion of optimistic humanism. It has had a monumental impact upon the life, social structure and political philosophy of China. Its founder Confucius lived in the fifth century B.C. Confucianism focuses on

Confucian temple in Kaohsiuna <u>Taiwan</u>, <u>Republic of</u>

the cultivation of virtue and maintenance of ethics, the most basic of which are *ren, yi,* and *li.* *Ren* is an obligation of altruism and humaneness for other individuals within a community, *yi* is the upholding of righteousness and the moral disposition to do good, and *li* is a system of norms and propriety that determines how a person should properly act within a community. Confucianism holds that one should give up one's life, if necessary, either passively or actively, for the sake of upholding the cardinal moral values of *ren* and *yi.* Although Confucius the man may have been a believer in Chinese folk religion, Confucianism as an ideology is humanistic and non-theistic, and does not involve a belief in the supernatural or in a personal god.

Cultures and countries strongly influenced by Confucianism include mainland China, Taiwan, Korea, Japan and Vietnam, as well as various territories settled predominantly by Chinese people, such as Singapore. Although Confucian ideas prevail in these areas, few people outside of academia identify themselves as Confucian, and instead see Confucian ethics as a complementary guideline for other ideologies and beliefs, including democracy, Marxism, capitalism, Islam, Buddhism and even Christianity. Confucius taught that man can save himself by following the way of the ancients. Christianity teaches that man does not have the capacity to save himself, but is in desperate need of a Savior. Confucius implied that human nature was basically good. Contrast this with what the Bible says:

> The heart is deceitful above all things, And desperately wicked; Who can know it? (Jer 17:9)

Laozi depicted as a Taoist

Taoism (modernly: **Daoism**) is a system of philosophy and religion based on the teachings of Lao-tze who was born in the sixth century B.C. in China. It emphasizes living in harmony with the Tao (modernly westernized as "Dao"). The term *Tao* means "way", "path" or "principle", and can also be found in Chinese philosophies and religions other than Taoism. In Taoism, however, *Tao* denotes something that is both the source and the driving force behind everything that exists.

exists. It is ultimately ineffable: "The Tao that can be told is not the eternal Tao."

Taoist philosophy proposes that the universe works harmoniously according to its own ways. There is the *yin*, or receptive aspect of the universe that expresses itself in silence, darkness, coolness and rest, and there is the *yang*, or active aspect of reality that expresses itself in speech, light and heat. When someone exerts their will

The Taijita, symbol of Taoism's yin & yang

against the world, they disrupt that harmony. Taoism asserts that one must place their will in harmony with the natural universe. Thus, a potentially harmful interference is to be avoided, and in this way, goals can be achieved effortlessly. Taoist propriety and ethics may vary depending on the particular school, but in general tends to emphasize <u>wu-wei</u> (action through non-action), "naturalness", simplicity, spontaneity, and the <u>Three Treasures</u>: compassion, moderation and humility. By *wu-wei*, the sage seeks to come into harmony with the great Tao, which itself is accomplished by non-action." The number of Taoists is difficult to estimate, due to a variety of factors including defining Taoism. Taoism does not fall under an umbrella or a definition of a single <u>organized religion</u>, but may be called a Chinese folk religion. The number of people practicing <u>Chinese folk religion</u> is estimated to be just under four hundred million. Most Chinese people and many others have been influenced in some way by Taoist tradition. Estimates for the number of Taoists worldwide range from twenty million and possibly to as many as 400 million in China alone.

Even though Tao may have a temporary appeal, such as with the "tune out, drop out" mentality of the 60's hippies in America, it ultimately cannot fulfill the needs of its disciples. <u>Jesus would have us get very involved with the world's problems in the power and love of God</u>. Contrast the personal God of the Bible with the "wu-wei" of Taoism:

> *Come to Me, all you who labor and are heavy laden, and I will give you rest. Take My yoke upon you and learn from Me, for I am gentle and lowly in heart, and you will find rest for your souls. For My yoke is easy and My burden is light* (Matt 11:28-30).

> *Go therefore and make disciples of all the nations, baptizing them in the name of the Father and of the Son and of the Holy Spirit, teaching them to observe all things that I have commanded you; and lo, I am with you always, even to the end of the age* (Matt 28:19-20).

But you shall receive power when the Holy Spirit has come upon you; and you shall be witnesses to Me in Jerusalem, and in all Judea and Samaria, and to the end of the earth (Acts 1:8).

Inasmuch then as the children have partaken of flesh and blood, He Himself likewise shared in the same, that through death He might destroy him who had the power of death, that is, the devil, and release those who through fear of death were all their lifetime subject to bondage....Therefore, in all things He had to be made like His brethren, that He might be a merciful and faithful High Priest in things pertaining to God, to make propitiation for the sins of the people. For in that He Himself has suffered, being tempted, He is able to aid those who are tempted (Heb 2:14-18).

Blessed be the God and Father of our Lord Jesus Christ, the Father of mercies and God of all comfort, who comforts us in all our tribulation, that we may be able to comfort those who are in any trouble, with the comfort with which we ourselves are comforted by God (2 Cor 1:3-4).

Moreover if your brother sins against you, go and tell him his fault between you and him alone. If he hears you, you have gained your brother. But if he will not hear, take with you one or two more, that by the mouth of two or three witnesses every word may be established. And if he refuses to hear them, tell it to the church. But if he refuses even to hear the church, let him be to you like a heathen and a tax collector. Assuredly, I say to you, whatever you bind on earth will be bound in heaven, and whatever you loose on earth will be loosed in heaven (Matt 18:15-18).

Ise Grand Shrine—Honden at Naiku. After 1871, it is the apex of the 80000 Shinto Shrines

Shintoism is a religion of Japan which venerates spirits in nature and of ancestors. Its origins can be traced to the 8th century BCE. It is devoid of any formal dogma. Fact books and statistics typically list some 80 to 90% of Japanese people as Shintoist. However polls suggest that most Japanese consider themselves non-religious and believe that there are currently only 4 million "actual" observers of Shinto in Japan. The vast majority of people in Japan who take part in Shinto rituals also practice <u>Buddhist</u> rituals. However Shinto does not actually require professing faith to be a believer or a practitioner. A person who practices "any" manner of Shinto rituals may be so counted, and as such it is difficult to query for exact figures based on self-identification of belief within Japan. Another problem is that Shinto is sometimes seen more as a way of life rather than a religion by the Japanese due to its long historical and cultural significance. Due to the syncretic nature of Shinto and Buddhism, most "life" events are handled by Shinto and "death" or "afterlife" events are handled by Buddhism. For example, it is typical in Japan to register or celebrate a birth at a Shinto shrine, while funeral arrangements are generally dictated by Buddhist tradition. The feudal Samurai soldier and the Kamikaze suicide fighter pilots of World War II emanated from Shintoism. The fact that Shinto in its purest form teaches the superiority of the Japanese people and their land above all others on earth is <u>diametrically opposed to the teaching of the Bible</u>.

As it is written: "There is none righteous, no, not one (Rom 3:10).

Then Peter opened his mouth and said: "In truth I perceive that God shows no partiality (Acts 10:34).

Zoroastrianism is a religion of Persia named for its founder Zoroaster and set forth in the Zend-Avesta which teaches the worship of Ormazd in the context of a struggle of the forces of light and of darkness, good and evil. Zoroastrians believe that there is one universal and transcendent God, <u>Ahura Mazda</u>. He is said to be the one uncreated Creator to whom all worship is ultimately directed. Ahura Mazda's creation – evident as *asha*, truth and order - is the <u>antithesis</u> of chaos, which is evident as *Druj* (falsehood and disorder). The resulting conflict involves the entire universe, including humanity, which has an active role to play in the conflict. The religion states that active participation in life through good deeds is necessary to ensure happiness and to keep chaos at bay.

Ahura Mazda will ultimately prevail over evil, at which point the universe will undergo a cosmic renovation and time will end. In the final renovation, all of creation - even the souls of the dead that were initially banished to "darkness" - will be reunited in Ahura Mazda, returning to life in the undead form. At the end of time, a savior-figure (a <u>Saoshyant</u>) will bring about a final renovation of the world (frasho kereti), in which the dead will be revived. In some form, it served as the national or <u>state religion</u> of a significant portion of the <u>Iranian people</u> for many centuries. The political power of the pre-Islamic Iranian dynasties lent

Zoroastrianism immense prestige in ancient times, and some of its leading doctrines were adopted by other religious systems. By one estimate, there are between 124,000 and 190,000 Zoroastrians worldwide. From this ancient empire we hear from the Hebrew prophet Daniel who gained a place of prominence through his interpretation of dreams and visions. The God of Zoroastrianism may at first seem similar to the God of the Bible, but he is thought to be a co-equal with *Angra Mainyu*, the god of evil, also eternal.

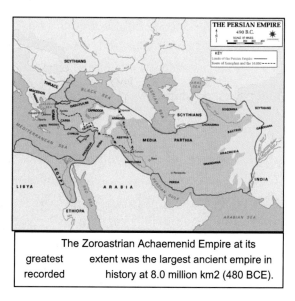

The Zoroastrian Achaemenid Empire at its greatest recorded extent was the largest ancient empire in history at 8.0 million km2 (480 BCE).

The God of the Bible is not co-equal with Satan. Satan is not the opposite of God; he is neither eternal nor all-powerful. The practice of Zoroastrianism involves much that is occultic and superstitious, something resoundingly condemned in the Scripture.

There shall not be found among you anyone who makes his son or his daughter pass through the fire, or one who practices witchcraft, or a soothsayer, or one who interprets omens, or a sorcerer, or one who conjures spells, or a medium, or a spiritist, or one who calls up the dead. For all who do these things are an abomination to the LORD, and because of these abominations the LORD your God drives them out from before you (Deut 18:10-12).

Worship in Zoroastrianism is legalistic and impersonal, reflecting the view of its impersonal god, Ahura Mazda. <u>In Christianity God is to be worshipped personally with all one's heart, since His nature is personal</u>.

A Psalm of Thanksgiving. Make a joyful shout to the LORD, all you lands! Serve the LORD with gladness; Come before His presence with singing. Know that the LORD, He is God; It is He who has made us, and not we ourselves; We are His people and the sheep of His pasture. Enter into His gates with thanksgiving, And into His courts with praise. Be thankful to Him, and bless His name. For the LORD is good; His mercy is everlasting, And His truth endures to all generations (Psalm 100).

The Bahá'i Faith is a monotheistic religion founded by Baháu'llah in 19th century BCE Persia. It emphasizes the spiritual unity of all mankind. There are an estimated 7.4 million Baha'is around the world in more than 200

Seat of the <u>Universal House of Justice</u>, governing body of the Bahá'ís, in <u>Haifa</u>, Israel

countries and territories. In the Bahá'I Faith, religious history is seen to have unfolded through a series of divine messengers, each of whom establish a religion that was suited to the needs of the time and the capacity of the people. These messengers have included Moses, Buddha, Jesus, Muhammad and Baháu'llah. Humanity is understood to be a process of collective evolution, and the need of the present time is for the establishment of peace, justice and unity on a global scale.

Contrast this with the <u>insights of the Bible's description of the deterioration leading to the end of time</u> which sounds more like progressive destruction than "collective evolution":

> The disciples asked Jesus, "Tell us, when will these things be, and what will be the sign of Your coming, and of the end of the age? (Matt 24:3)

In answer to their question the following is paraphrased from Matthew 24:37-38; Luke 18:8; 2 Peter 3:3-4; 1 Timothy 4:1-3; and 2 Timothy 3:1-5; 4:3-4:

> Just as in the days of Noah before the flood people will be eating, drinking and marrying as if nothing were wrong, then Christ will suddenly come. Difficult times will come because men will be lovers of money, boastful, arrogant, revilers, disobedient to parents, ungrateful, unholy, unloving, irreconcilable, malicious gossips, without self-control, brutal, haters of good, treacherous, reckless, conceited, lovers of pleasure rather than lovers of God. It will be difficult to find faith on the earth. They would rather pay attention to deceitful spirits and doctrines of demons, by means of hypocrisy of liars seared in their own conscience as with a branding iron, men who forbid marriage, advocate abstaining from foods, which God has created to be gratefully shared in by those who believe and know the truth. They will not endure sound doctrine; but wanting to have their ears tickled, they will accumulate for themselves teachers in accordance to their own desires; and will turn away their ears from the truth, and will turn

aside to myths. Mockers will come with their mocking, following after their own lusts, and saying, 'Where is the promise of His coming? For ever since the fathers fell asleep, all continues as it was from the beginning of creation.'

CHAPTER 10
JUDAISM AND THE PROMISE-PLAN OF GOD

Judaism is traced to Abraham and having its spiritual and ethical principles embodied chiefly in the biblical Old Testament and in the Talmud. Judaism is the

The Western Wall in Jerusalem is a remnant of the wall encircling the Second Temple. The Temple Mount is the holiest site in Judaism.

covenantal relationship God established with the Children of Israel. Judaism holds that God revealed His laws and commandments to Moses on Mount Sinai in the form of both the Written and Oral Torah. Unlike other ancient Near Eastern gods, the Hebrew God is portrayed as unitary and solitary; consequently, the Hebrew God's principal relationships are not with other gods, but with the world, and more specifically, with the people He created. Judaism thus begins with an ethical monotheism: the belief that God is one, and concerned with the actions of humankind. According to the Hebrew Bible, God promised Abraham to make of his offspring a great nation. God commanded the nation of Israel to love and worship only one God. The Jewish nation is to reciprocate God's concern for the world in their love for one another, the imitation of God's love for people. These commandments are but two of a large corpus of commandments and laws that constitute this covenant, which is the substance of Judaism.

Christianity is built upon Judaism. Without it there is no Jesus. Jesus *"came to His own, and those who were His own did not receive Him. But as many as received Him, to them He gave the right to become children of God, even to those who believe in His name"* (John 1:11-12). Those that did believe, whether Old Testament or New Testament saints, Jew or Gentile, received the promises of God. Israel is referred to in Scripture as "chosen." "Chosen" is understood in terms of bringing Christ to the world... Christ through whom all the world is blessed. Judaism is incomplete without the coming of the Messiah, Yeshua. Christianity thus fulfills Judaism.

> Do not think that I came to abolish the Law or the
> Prophets; I did not come to abolish, but to fulfill (Jesus
> in Matt 5:17).

Walter Kaiser Jr. has argued that the "promise–plan" of God holds consistently through the Old and New Testaments as the plan unfolds in detail while never changing in direction and purpose. The "new covenant" prophesied in Jeremiah and the "New Testament" do not so much supersede the former covenants with Israel as renew them. As God's plan unfolds through Israel, the old covenants are retained and progressively enriched, enlarged and incorporated into a body of foundational truths that carry the main burden of the whole message and plan of the Bible. The Christian Church does not have an independent existence or genesis of its own, as if it had no roots and no history, for in that case it would be devoid of all association, rootage, or previous contacts. Its nourishment and sustenance comes from the promise roots embedded in the words given to the patriarchs and to the nation Israel. [51]

Think of the beliefs we share or which originate from Judaism:[52]

- In the belief in one God our Father
- In the hope of His salvation
- In ignorance of His ways
- In humility before His omnipotence
- In the knowledge that we belong to Him, not He to us
- In love and reverence for God
- In doubt about our wavering fidelity
- In the paradox that we are dust and yet the image of God
- In the consciousness that God wants us as partners in the sanctification of the world
- In the condemnation of arrogant religious chauvinism
- In the conviction that love of God is crippled without love of neighbor
- In knowledge that on our way to Him all speech about God must remain as stammering

For you are all sons of God through faith in Christ Jesus. For as many of you as were baptized into Christ have put on Christ. There is neither Jew nor Greek, there is neither slave nor free, there is neither male nor female; for you are all one in Christ Jesus. And if you are Christ's, then you are Abraham's seed, and heirs according to the promise (Gal 3:26-29).

What's So Special about the Jews?

Many years ago a man in my Sunday school class asked me, "What's so important about the Jews?" I gave him the best answer I had. "The Jews brought us Jesus and Jesus was a Jew." But, neither he nor I were satisfied with that answer. If one is to make peace with the value of Judaism, the Church, the covenant relationships described in the Bible and the mind of God, then he should do it by dealing with the actual biblical text and not by forcing a favored presumptive theology on these issues.

The Scriptures show that God revealed Himself through Abraham and the Mosaic covenant as the one true God for all mankind. Thus began the covenantal relationship with a chosen people, the Jews. Let me suggest that the best way of looking at the big picture as presented by Scripture, is to understand that there is a single Promise [53] beginning with God's curse of the serpent: "he shall bruise your head, and you shall bruise his heal" (Gen 3:15), detailed in Abraham that he would be the father of many nations, that God would give his heirs a homeland and that through him all the world would be blessed (Gen 12:2-3), that God's strongest desire was to tabernacle with His people as put forward through Moses (Exo 29:43-46), further defined in David (that he would be a king forever through his heirs (2 Sam 7:12-19) and carried forward by the prophets and fulfilled in Jesus Christ. Jesus Christ is, indeed, King of the Jews. Yet, because of their rejection of Him, the Jews have been cut off for a time and Gentiles grafted in to the Olive Tree which is a place of blessing for the whole world. This is the Church. But, the Church will one day be removed as they will be caught up to meet Him in the air. That event will mark the beginning of the end. The promise is that all Israel will eventually be saved as they are grafted back in to the source of the blessing, that is, Christ Jesus. Along with them a great multitude will be saved during the Tribulation through the evangelism of the Jews. Finally, Jew and Gentile, every tribe and nation, will be gathered together in the presence of God and of His Christ forever.

While there is a New Covenant as prophesied by Jeremiah 31:31-34 and confirmed by Hebrews 8:6-13, it is best understood as the continuation of God's marvelous promise rather than a new dispensation. I am not a proponent of "replacement theology," whereby Israel is superseded by the church due to its failure to receive Christ. Paul makes this clarification to the Galatians:

> *Now to Abraham and his Seed were the promises made. He does not say, "And to seeds," as of many, but as of one, "And to your Seed," who is Christ. And this I say, that the law, which was four hundred and thirty years later, cannot annul the covenant that was confirmed before by God in Christ, that it should make the promise of no effect. For if the inheritance is of the law, it is no longer of promise; but God gave it to Abraham by promise* (Gal 16-18). *For there is no distinction between Jew and Greek, for the same Lord over all is rich to all who call upon Him. For "whoever calls on the name of the LORD shall be saved* (Rom 10:12-13).

With the death and resurrection of Christ, as prophesied, the last days have already begun. With His advent the hope of all the ages, the full expression and reality of God's love and holiness have been made known.

The Covenants of the Old Testament

Jesus said to the Samaritan woman at the well, "Salvation is of the Jews" (John 4:22b). To those outside of Judaism Jesus said, "You worship what you do not know" (John 4:22a). God commanded the Jews not only to put no other gods before Him, but he disallowed worship of these gods on Jewish soil. He told the Jews not to intermarry and not to allow foreign gods to be brought into the land. But, let's start at the very beginning.

The Edenic (Adamic) Covenant - promising redemption

Genesis 3:14-15

From the beginning of mankind God implemented a covenant relationship with humanity: "And the Lord commanded the man, saying, "You may surely eat of every tree of the garden, but of the tree of the knowledge of good and evil you shall not eat, for the day that you eat of it you shall surely die" (Gen 2:16-17). Of course, Adam and Eve broke this covenant resulting in God's curse and expulsion from Eden. From this original disobedience sin came into the world and upon every man born of Adam and Eve. Yet, a prophecy given while God addressed the serpent brought a promise of redemption:

I will put enmity between you and the woman, and between your offspring and her offspring; he shall bruise your head, and you shall bruise his heel (Gen 3:15).

The Noachian Covenant - preserving the race

Genesis 9:8-13

Many generations after, God looked at mankind and observed that the wickedness of man was great on the earth. What's more, every intention of the thoughts of his heart was only evil continually. The Lord regretted that he had made man on the earth, and it grieved His heart. God decided to "blot out man from the face of the earth." Nevertheless, "Noah found grace in the eyes of the Lord" (Gen 6:8). God instructed Noah to build a huge boat for the safety of his family and the many animals. After the great flood and catastrophic upheaval of the whole earth, God made a covenant with Noah: "I will never again curse the ground because of man, for the intention of man's heart is evil from his youth. Neither will I ever again strike down every living creature as I have done. While the earth remains, seedtime and harvest, cold and heat, summer and winter, day and night, shall not cease.... I will require a reckoning for the life of man.... And you, be fruitful and multiply, increase greatly on the earth and multiply in it.... Behold I establish my covenant with you, that never again shall there be a flood to destroy the earth" (Gen 8:21-9:11). Humanity was guaranteed survival through the Noachian Covenant. Nations were born from Noah's family.

The Abrahamic Covenant – granting blessing through a people
Genesis 15:3-6, 18-21

From the land of Ur (Mesopotamia), God called Abram to a land that God would later reveal. In unfolding covenants God promised Abram land (Gen 12:1,7), blessing (12:2), protection (12:3) and the realization of a great nation through Abram (12:2). God narrows his covenant at this point so that it is with a specific people. The blessing of Abram is validated through Melchizedek, the king of Salem (Jerusalem), and "priest of the God most high," that God would make them a great nation, that they would receive a homeland and that the whole world would be blessed through them was renewed with Isaac and Jacob as the twelve tribes of Israel brought the one true and living God to the world through Abraham.

The Mosaic (Sinaitic) Covenant – designating Israel as God's chosen people

Exodus 19:5-8

Leading the Jewish people out from Egyptian slavery Moses renewed and brought definition to God's covenant. Moses descended from Sinai with the Ten Commandments reflecting the glory and holiness of God. He dealt immediately with the idolatry of the people. That God's strongest desire was to dwell with His people was developed in Moses (Exo 29:43-46). Over the next generation through the miracles and protection of God and in their pursuit of the Promised Land given by God, the Israelites are prepared to receive that land in conjunction with all of the covenant of God. "Choose you this day whom you will serve," was Joshua's challenge as he led them across the Jordan.

The Levitical Covenant – reconciling to God through priestly atonement

Leviticus 17:11; Numbers 25:10-13

For the life of the flesh is in the blood, and I have given it for you on the altar to make atonement for your souls (Lev 17:11).

Phinehas the son of Eleazar, son of Aaron the priest, has turned back my wrath from the people of Israel, in that he was jealous with my jealousy among them, so that I did not consume the people of Israel in my jealousy. Therefore say, "Behold, I give to him my covenant of peace, and it shall be to him and to his descendants after him the covenant of a perpetual priesthood, because he was jealous for his God and made atonement for the people of Israel (Num 25:10-13).

The Levitical Covenant seems to fall wholly under the Mosaic Covenant and to a certain degree acts as an extension of it. A very special relationship between God and the tribe of the Levites, a special calling and privilege was given to them to live in service to the temple or tabernacle. A clan given to holiness, they were functionaries of the public ceremonial law giving sacrifice on behalf of Israel.

The Davidic Covenant – salvation through David's dynasty

Psalm 89:3-4

The Lord revealed to David that he would be a king forever through his heirs (2 Sam 7:12-19). This promise was carried forward through the prophets and fulfilled in Jesus Christ. We can see the blood line from the tribe of Judah through David to Jesus. Jeremiah 23:5-6 describes the branch of David and can be compared to Matthew's presentation of Jesus as the Davidic Messiah. Not only was the prophecy regarding David fulfilled but the promise to Abraham that through him all the world would be blessed. Luke explains it like this: God "raised up for them David as king, to whom also He gave testimony and said, 'I Have found David the son of Jesse, a man after My own heart, who will do all My will.' From this seed, according to the promise, God raised up for Israel a Savior – Jesus" (Acts 13:22-23).

Although these are expressed as Old Testament "covenants," they are best understood as a single promise-plan to bring salvation through the Jew to all mankind. There has not failed one word of all He promised (1 Kings 8:56; Joshua 21:45). The Old Testament covenants point toward the New.

As the Bible unfolds this promise of blessing, four reasons for why God chose and created Israel are discernable. These are the purposes for which He chose them:[54]

1. First, they are to receive, write, and preserve the Word of God. As the Apostle Paul testified, "They were entrusted with the oracles of God."

2. Second, the way God deals with Israel in response to their faith or lack of faith is a living historical lesson about God's character. The way God dealt with Israel as a nation teaches principles of how He deals with the individual who believes in Him.

3. Third, the Jews are to be the physical race through which the Messiah the Savior of the world would be born. Isaiah predicted the mission of this Messiah, "It is too small a thing that You should be My Servant to raise up the tribes of Jacob, and to restore the preserved ones of Israel; I will also make You a light to the Gentiles so that My salvation may reach to the end of the earth.

4. Fourth, Israel is called to spread the message of the true God and His salvation to the world.

THE NEW COVENANT

...But the Lord will arise over you, and His glory will be seen upon you. The Gentiles shall come to your light... (Isaiah 60:2-3)

The New Covenant is the capstone of the promise-plan of God. It is no wonder that the very first words in the New Testament are *"The book of the genealogy of Jesus Christ, the Son of David, the Son of Abraham"* (Matt 1:1). While Christ was present in both type and form in the Old Testament, it was not until His incarnation that He was fully human as well as fully divine. The Word became flesh and dwelt among us, and we beheld His glory, the glory as of the only begotten of the Father, full of grace and truth (John 1:14). He came unto his own, and his own received him not. But as many as received him, to them he gave the power to become the sons of God, even to them that believe on his name (John 1:11-12). He is the image of the invisible God, the firstborn over all creation (Col 1:15). However, He did not consider it robbery to be equal with God, but made Himself of no reputation, taking on the form of a bondservant, and coming in the likeness of men. He humbled Himself and became obedient to the point of death, even the death of the cross (Phil 2:6-8). This condescension ushered in the New Covenant prophesied by Jeremiah:

> *Behold, the days come, saith the LORD, that I will make a new covenant with the house of Israel, and with the house of Judah: Not according to the covenant that I made with their fathers in the day that I took them by the hand to bring them out of the land of Egypt; which my covenant they brake, although I was an husband unto them, saith*

the LORD: *But this shall be the covenant that I will make with the house of Israel; After those days, saith the* LORD, *I will put my law in their inward parts, and write it in their hearts; and will be their God, and they shall be my people. And they shall teach no more every man his neighbor, and every man his brother, saying, Know the* LORD: *for they shall all know me, from the least of them unto the greatest of them, saith the* LORD: *for I will forgive their iniquity, and I will remember their sin no more* (Jer 31:31-34).

The New Covenant was based on the sacrificial blood of Jesus. He said as He shared the first communion with His disciples, "This is my blood of the new testament, which is shed for many for the remission of sins" (Matt 26:28). But this was not to be yet another legal requirement given to men in order to be saved; it was characterized by a work of the Holy Spirit:

But ye are not in the flesh, but in the Spirit, if so be that the Spirit of God dwell in you. Now if any man have not the Spirit of Christ, he is none of his. And if Christ be in you, the body is dead because of sin; but the Spirit is life because of righteousness. But if the Spirit of Him that raised up Jesus from the dead dwell in you, he that raised up Christ from the dead shall also quicken your mortal bodies by his Spirit that dwelleth in you. Therefore, brethren, we are debtors, not to the flesh, to live after the flesh (Rom 8:9-12).

This new covenant was to be a matter not of the letter, but of the Spirit. And its truth was to be "written on the heart." Hebrews confirmed the New Covenant of Jeremiah: "For this is the covenant that I will make with the house of Israel after those days, saith the Lord; I will put my laws into their mind, and write them in their hearts: and I will be to them a God, and they shall be to me a people" (Heb 8:10).

Hebrews Chapter 9 makes it clear that this New Covenant was to be made with Judah and Israel (a reflection of the divided and idolatrous kingdom). The earthly had become a mere foreshadowing of the heavenly covenant. The sacrifice of animals for the remission of sin had been replaced by the precious blood of Christ, the Lamb of God who takes away the sins of the world. And that sacrifice had been made once and for all time. The Sinaitic covenant's ceremonial aspects were only "copies," "patterns," or "shadows" of the real that had come. However, it would be wrong to think that just because the sacrificial system had been replaced, therefore the Ten Commandments (moral law Exod 20; Deut 5) and the Holiness Code (Lev 18-20), had been replaced.[55]

I will make an everlasting covenant with them, that I will not turn away from doing them good; but I will put My fear in their hearts so that they will not depart from Me (Jer 32:40).

We can see that the Old Testament foreshadows so completely the coming of Christ that the Gospel can be taught without the aid of the New Testament. Perhaps the foretelling is completed in Jeremiah 31:31-34 where the prophet looks forward to the New Covenant. It is not so much that the New Covenant is complicated or difficult for us to understand; it is that it is so profound we scarce can take it in. The Old Covenant was of the Letter of the Law given to Moses and administered through the oft repeated priestly ritual for the covering of sins as a copy of the true sacrifice. The New Covenant is by the true mediation of the Blood of Jesus Christ, the sacrifice once and for all for the remission of sins, written on the minds and hearts of the believers through the eternal Spirit.

KING OF THE JEWS

Consider now for whom Jesus came? Of course, He came for the whole world. But, Jesus first came to His own. There were individual Jews who received and accepted Him as the promised Messiah, but in general, and in fulfilment of prophecy, they "knew Him not." Yet, this is nothing new, for God had so often given His news, His warning, His promises through prophets, even though God knew their word would not be received.

> *Go and say to the people: Keep on hearing, but do not understand; keep on seeing, but do not perceive. Make the heart of this people dull, and their ears heavy, and blind their eyes; lest they see with their eyes, and hear with their ears, and understand with their hearts, and turn and be healed (Isa 6:9-10).*

Still, God was faithful, merciful and resolute in His desire to save. His promises to Abraham, to Moses and to David would be kept. He would bring to Israel an everlasting king. This would be the promised Messiah. Isaiah put it this way:

> For a child will be born to us, a son will be given to us; and the government will rest on His shoulders; and His name will be called Wonderful Counselor, Mighty God, Eternal Father, Prince of Peace. There will be no end to the increase of his government or of Peace, on the throne of David and over His kingdom, to establish it and to uphold it with justice and righteousness from then on and forevermore. The zeal of the Lord of hosts will accomplish this (Isa 9:6-7).

It is "to us," i.e. to Israel, that a child will be born and a son will be given. Obviously, the God of Israel is the One who will give this son to His people. This child will be a ruler in Israel. It is on David's throne, that of the King of Israel, that He will sit. It is over David's kingdom that Messiah reigns. It is David's kingdom that Messiah establishes and upholds. Messiah, whom God will give to Israel, is David's son (Isaiah began to prophesy in the reign of Uzziah, a tenth generation descendant of David."[56] The New Covenant was first for the Jew. Jeremiah's prophecy was given to the Jewish remnant in the days of captivity promising that Judah would be saved and Israel would dwell securely; and this is His name by which He will be called, "The Lord our righteousness" (Jer 23:5-6). But Jeremiah's prophecy was given just before the Babylonians destroyed Jerusalem and put an end to the Davidic kings. The Lord was promising that He would yet raise up a Branch, i.e. a descendent of David, a root, to be king. He will rule as David did, over a united kingdom – "Judah will be saved, and Israel will dwell securely."

This Son of David is the salvation and security of the Jewish people. The gospel begins with the genealogy of Jesus from Abraham, through David to Bethlehem. The New Covenant scriptures begin with this genealogy because it is indispensable. It is not out of place. Without this Jewish genealogy, there is no Messiah, there is no gospel. That is why the Lord put it first.[57] To the virgin Mary the angel announced His birth:

> *You shall name Him Jesus. He will be great, and will be called the Son of the Most High; and the Lord God will give Him the throne of His father David; and He will reign over the house of Jacob forever; and his kingdom will have no end* (Luke 1:27,30-33).

Luke records that the Holy Spirit filled Zechariah, the father of John the Baptist, and he prophesied, saying,

> *Blessed be the Lord God of Israel, for He has visited us and accomplished redemption for His people, and has raised up a horn of salvation for us in the house of David his servant, as He spoke by the mouth of his holy prophets from of old, salvation from our enemies, and from the hand of all who hate us; to show mercy toward our fathers, and to remember His holy covenant, the oath which He swore to Abraham our father, to grant us that we being delivered from the hand of our enemies might serve Him without fear in holiness and righteousness before Him all our days* (Luke 1:67-75).

In Romans Paul makes it clear that the New Covenant is made with the Jewish people:

They are Israelites, and to them belong the adoption, the glory, the covenants, the giving of the law, the worship, and the promises. To them belong the patriarchs, and from their race, according to the flesh, is the Christ, who is God over all, blessed forever. Amen (Rom 9:4-5).

With these and many other references from the biblical text it would be difficult to argue, as some have done, that the New Covenant was given to the church. Without doubt, though not the direct recipient, the church is included as a benefactor of the New Covenant. Through the New Covenant the Gentiles were blessed and were grafted into the Olive Tree, the place of blessing. It was always God's kind intention to bless the whole world through Abraham. Paul explained that despite Israel's disobedience, God's dealings with the nation had not ended. God's disapproval, resulting in their being set aside, was temporary. God would fulfill all His promises at the proper time despite their disobedience.[58] God has a future plan for national Israel independent and apart from his work of forming the Church, the body of Christ.

GENTILES GRAFTED INTO THE OLIVE TREE

When Mary and Joseph brought the boy Jesus to the temple to present him to the Lord, they were met by a devout Jew, Simeon, who took the child in his arms and said,

"Lord, now You are letting Your servant depart in peace, According to Your word; For my eyes have seen Your salvation Which You have prepared before the face of all peoples, A light to bring revelation to the Gentiles, And the glory of Your people Israel." (Luke 2:29-32).

According to Simeon, Jesus was a light to the Gentiles and the glory of Israel. Isaiah had prophesied, *"It is too small a thing that you should be My Servant to raise up the tribes of Jacob and to restore the preserved ones of Israel; I will also make you as a light for the nations, that my salvation may reach to the end of the earth"* (Isa 49:6). Paul and Barnabas reminded the Gentile citizens of Antioch of this reality. When they heard this, it says they began rejoicing and glorifying the word of the Lord, and as many as were appointed to eternal life believed. As a result, the disciples were filled with joy and with the Holy Spirit.

> *He would be the first to rise from the dead, and would proclaim light to the Jewish people and to the Gentiles (Acts 26:22-23). For there is no distinction between Jew and Greek, for the same Lord over all is rich to all who call upon Him. For whoever calls on the name of the Lord shall be saved (Rom 10:12-13)*

But the Jews incited a persecution against Paul and Barnabas, and drove them out of their district (Acts 13:44-52). Because of their unbelief, the Jews are described as branches broken off from the olive tree. But the olive tree is the promise of God and the source of salvation to the whole world. The olive tree is the fulfillment of God's promise to national Israel in the Messiah, that through this olive tree all the world would be blessed. During this time of blessing, this day of grace, this age of the Church, the Gentile has received mercy. *"Once you were not a people, but now you are God's people; once you had not received mercy, but now you have received mercy"* (1 Pet 2:10). For now, explained Paul, *"a partial hardening has come upon Israel, until the fullness of the Gentiles has come in"* (Rom 11:25). Yet, there is always a Jewish remnant who believes. *"There is neither Jew nor Greek, there is neither slave nor free, there is no male and female, for you are all one in Christ Jesus,"* explained Paul to the Galatian Christians (Gal 3:28). In the program God revealed to Israel, Gentiles could be blessed only through a relationship or association with Israel. In God's program of the Church, the body of Christ, both Jews and Gentiles are blessed by believing the gospel of grace by faith (1 Cor 15:1-4).

What then will be "the fullness of the Gentiles"? We do not know the time, but it will end with the removal of the Church (the Rapture). During the time of tribulation God will appoint two witnesses (Rev 11:1-4) and then 144,000 sealed evangelists (Rev 7) which will issue in the promise of God that "all Israel will be saved."

> *For if you were cut off from what is by nature a wild olive tree, and were grafted contrary to nature into a cultivated olive tree, how much more will these who are the natural branches be grafted into their own olive tree?* (Rom 11:22-24)

ALL ISRAEL WILL BE SAVED ALONG WITH A GREAT MULTITUDE FROM EVERY NATION

Once the church is removed, the miracle will begin. The gospel of the kingdom and repentance will again be preached to the Jews. But, this time, they will be responsive. Why? Because their heart of stone has been replaced by a heart of flesh. God's promise will be fulfilled: that He will make an everlasting covenant with Israel, that He will not turn away from doing them good, but will put His fear in their hearts so that they will not depart from Him. A "new covenant" with God will be realized by Israel, not like the Mosaic, but the law will be put within them, written on their hearts. Finally, Jehovah will be their God and they will be His people. Unlike at the time of the first advent, they will know Him "from the least of them to the greatest, declares the Lord. For I will forgive their iniquity, and I will remember their sin no more" (Jer 31:31-34). Ezekiel confirms this good news:

> I will restore the fortunes of Jacob and have mercy on the whole house of Israel, and I will be jealous for my holy name. They shall forget their shame and all the treachery they have practiced against me, when they dwell securely in their land with none to make them afraid (Eze 39:25-26).

Paul brings this understanding: that "all Israel will be saved" (Rom 11:26). Quoting Isaiah 27:9 and 59:29 Paul explains that a Redeemer will come from Zion and remove all ungodliness from Jacob. He will establish a [new] covenant with them and take away their sins. Does this mean every single Jew in the flesh? That will remain a mystery for now. Does the New Covenant apply to the Church? That is made obvious by Hebrews chapter 8. And it is best explained by Paul's grafting into the olive tree discussed above. But it is given to the Jews and will be made complete during the great tribulation.

In the Revelation given to John, after the 144,000 Jews are sealed, John sees a great multitude that no one could number, from every nation, from all tribes and peoples and languages, standing before the throne and before the Lamb. These are the redeemed coming out of the great tribulation. Are these the result of the evangelism of the Two Witnesses and of the 144,000? They are not the Church, for it has been removed. But these redeemed will include those Jews who are made whole through the blood of the Lamb.

The New Covenant of Jeremiah will not be fully accomplished until the second advent of Christ and the Millennial Kingdom, for it is there that the Kingdom of promise will be fully established. It is there that the government of Christ will be fully "on His shoulder" (Isa 9:6). It is there that the "righteous branch" springing up from David will execute righteousness and judgment in the land (Jer 33:15). It is then that the dragon (the devil Satan) will be bound for a thousand years that he might not deceive the nations (Rev 20:4-5). It is there that the martyrs of the tribulation will be resurrected to rule with Christ for a thousand years (Rev 4-5). It is there that God will bring back Israel from the east and west to live again in Jerusalem (Zech 8:7-8). There the nations will no longer mock and despise Israel (Zech 8:3). God will reverse the curse on nature as the vine and the field produce and the heavens send down their dew (Zech 8:12). It is here that the Messiah will restore Jerusalem, the city of Zion, a teaching and worship center for the whole earth.

> Great is the LORD, and greatly to be praised in the city of our God, in His holy mountain. Beautiful in elevation, the joy of the whole earth, is Mount Zion on the sides of the north, the city of the great King (Psa 48:1-2).

The writer of the epistle to the Hebrews reminds these Jewish Christians that in contrast to their ancestors during the time of Moses who could not bear the presence and direct message of God, and would not dare even touch the mount where God spoke with Moses, that they having been made ready in Christ have returned to hear the word of Jesus without fear (Heb 12:22-24):

> But you have come to Mount Zion and to the city of the living God, the heavenly Jerusalem, to an innumerable company of angels, to the general assembly and church of the firstborn who are registered in heaven, to God the Judge of all, to the spirits of just men made perfect, to Jesus the Mediator of the new covenant, and to the blood of sprinkling that speaks better things than that of Abel.

For He is the radiance of the glory of God... and upholds the universe by the word of his power (Heb 1:3). More than all the dwellings of Jacob (Psa 87:2-3), more than the city of David   (2 Sam 5:7), more than the location of Solomon's temple, more than the nation of Israel (Zech 9:13), Zion has become the city of the living God, the Zion of the Holy One of Israel (Isa 60:14). The kingdom of the world has become the kingdom of our Lord and of His Christ, and He shall reign forever and ever (Rev 11:15b).

We have shown that there is a single promise-plan for salvation and that the Old Covenant points to the New. The Old is set aside because of the New. We have shown that Israel remains a chosen nation until the completion of all things. What's so important about the Jews? They are God's chosen people, chosen to bring us not only the world's only true God and the amazing Word of God in its history, law, poetry and prophecy, but God's promise-plan to bring us

Jesus the Christ. The gospel of Jesus Christ can be learned and taught from the Old Testament of the Jews without reference to the New Testament. It shows that God always had in mind the promise of redemption to the whole world. With the first Advent of Christ, the Law and Prophets were fulfilled in part. But, his own Jewish people largely rejected Him. With the Day of Pentecost God's plan brought about the Church.

I will build My church, and the gates of Hades shall not prevail against it (Matt 16:18).

We have endeavored to answer the question, "What's so important about the Jews?" Now, we have to ask what is so important about the Church? It includes every nation, tribe and tongue. But the Church is grafted to the Olive Tree which is the promise of God and the source of salvation to the whole world that came by Christ through Abraham. There are many Jewish Christians today, but one day all of Israel will come to believe in Jesus the Messiah, the fulfillment of all the Law and the Prophets. They will be grafted back into that Olive Tree from which they were cut off. Why will they come to believe? ...because of the New Covenant that God has made with them. This is the culmination of God's plan for mankind. Jew and Gentile alike will worship in the temple which is the Lord God Almighty and the Lamb in the New Jerusalem.

CHAPTER 11

THE SPIRIT OF IDOLATRY

You shall have no other gods before Me. You shall not make for yourself a carved image or any likeness of anything that is in heaven above or that is on the earth beneath or that is in the water below. You shall not bow down to them or serve them, for I, the Lord, your God, am a jealous god, responding to the transgression of fathers by dealing with children to the third and fourth generations of those who reject me, and showing covenant faithfulness to a thousand generations of those who love me and keep my commandments (Exod 20:3-6).

For the nominal believer idolatry must be preceded by apostasy, that is forsaking the God of the Bible. W.E. McCumber, in his devotional book *Was It Not I? And Other Questions God Asks*, treats one of these questions from Jeremiah 2:11. The question God asked through Jeremiah is, "Has a nation ever changed its gods?" Here Israel had changed the glory of God for worthless idols. Idolatry followed the forsaking of their God. What is an idol? asks McCumber. Anyone or anything to which persons assign the place and value that God should have in their affections and activities is an idol. "People are choking on dust who could be drinking from a spring that never stops flowing."[59]

Idolatry is the construction of man-made images for worship, to which one bows down, treats as god, especially after having rejected the true and living God. That is the treatment in the Old Testament. The Hebrew people spent four centuries in Egypt. With the Exodus they left behind the many gods of Egyptian mythology. Anubis (god of the dead), Anuket and Hapi (goddess and god of the river Nile), Geb (god of the earth), Nut (goddess of sky and stars, Ra (god of the sun), Osiris (god of the underworld and the afterlife) and over a hundred more were worshiped and appeased through temple offerings and ritual. It brought great shame to the Israelites as they impatiently constructed a golden calf for worship in Moses' absence. The familiar perhaps became a comfort to them in their uncertainty even though they knew very well that the Lord God had brought them out of Egypt and had revealed Himself at Mount Sinai. While Moses received the Law from God, God halted the process. He told Moses to quickly descend because the people had made for themselves a golden calf and bowed down to it and sacrificed to it. God expressed His anger to Moses; "I have seen this people. Look what a stiff-necked people they are! So now, leave me alone so that my anger can burn against them and I can destroy them..." (Exod 32:9-10). But Moses sought the favor of the Lord and the Lord relented. Moses descended the mountain and dealt with the sin. Yet, God sent a plague so that the people would suffer the consequences of their sin. In fact, none of these complaining idolatrous people entered the Promised Land 40 years hence. As one reads the Old Testament, it is clear that God hated the sin of idolatry. It is no wonder that it is defined by the first two commandments.

I have noticed that these commandments have been broadened in type to include **putting any "thing" before God**. That certainly describes an idolatrous spirit, but I am reticent to call so many things "idolatry". When one tries to make it mean everything, it ends up meaning nothing. Idolatry seems less of an issue in the New Testament although there is the issue of eating meat offered to idols (1 Cor 8-10). When John warns Christians, "Little children, guard yourselves from idols" (1 John 5:21), the context suggests guarding against false teachings. Realize that you are in Christ, and do not be subject to anything but that which is true.

I am not sure that it is good exegesis to equate idolatry with passion for a hobby, sports team or the love of any other subject of interest. Yet, it is interesting that some upon conversion feel they must give up those things associated with the old life. One man I knew gave up his fiddle which he used to play with the Sons of the Pioneers in his unconverted life. Another man I know gave up rock and roll music which had been his obsession before he was saved. Although I found these sacrifices odd, I admired the determination of each to put God first and not allow any former passion to drag them back into the old life.

Nor am I so sure of A.W. Tozer's definition of idolatry as **"the entertainment of thoughts about God that are unworthy of Him."** [60] Here the idea is that the germination of idolatry is rooted in a diluted understanding of God, undervaluing His worthiness, dismissing his holiness, disregarding His love, diluting His truth or forgetting His jealousy.

Others see modern-day idolatry as a "dark exchange." Men construct idols when their affections drift away from the exclusive worship He requires. Here there is a dark exchange of one for the other as if man will inevitably worship someone or something even if he does not worship the Living God. Tozer said that "An idol of the mind is as offensive to God as an idol of the hand." D.L. Moody declared, "You don't have to go to heathen lands today to find false gods. America is full of them. Whatever you love more than God is your idol." [61] John MacArthur affirms, "Idolatry is having any false god – any object, idea, philosophy, habit, occupation, sport, or whatever that has one's primary concern and loyalty or that to any degree decreases one's trust in and loyalty to the Lord." [62]

Romans 1 follows this idea of exchanging something for God:

> For since the creation of the world his invisible attributes – his eternal power and divine nature – have been clearly seen, because they are understood through what has been made. So people are without excuse. For although they knew God, they did not glorify Him as God or give Him thanks, but they became futile in their thoughts and their senseless hearts were darkened. Although they claimed to be wise, they became fools and exchanged the glory of the immortal God for an image resembling mortal human beings or birds or four-footed animals or reptiles. Therefore God gave them over in the desires of their hearts to impurity, to dishonor their bodies among themselves. They exchanged the truth of God for a lie and worshiped and served the creation rather than the Creator, who is blessed forever! Amen (Rom 1:20-24).

"Don't be swayed by the false values and goals of this world, but put Christ and his will first in everything you do" (Billy Graham).

Daniel Henderson gives this list: [63]

- When we find greater delight in our hobbies than in our walk with Christ, we are wandering down the path of idolatry.
- When we spend more time absorbing the entertainment of Hollywood than we do contemplating godly truth, we are toying with idolatry.

- When any possession dominates our thoughts and captures our affections more than the treasure of Christ, it has likely become an idol.
- When social media excites us more than spiritual interests, we are in the process of erecting other gods.
- When we find excessive delight in a relationship with some other person to the neglect of our relationship with Christ, that person can become an idol.
- When we find more delight in serving Christ than in seeking Christ, even ministry can become an idol. William Secker commented, "I would neither have you be idle in duties – nor make an idol of duties."
- When we find greater confidence in our own strengths and capabilities than in a humble reliance on Christ, we can easily fall under the spell of the idolatry of self-worship.

Walter Kaiser Jr. put it this way: "When any form of leisure or entertainment competes for the believer's time and loyalties, equaling or exceeding the time and joy that he gives and receives from spiritual things, then he has crossed the line and entered headlong into idolatry."[64]

Paul seemingly broadened the scope of idolatry for Christians when he identified covetousness with idolatry (Col 3:5-6). Obviously, idolatry here is associated with "earnest desire". **Idolatry then is covetous desire**. Jesus said that the covetous man will not be "rich toward God."(Luke 12:13-21). In Ephesians Paul saw the covetous man as idolatrous because he denies his faith in God and scorns His values.

Many pastors and teachers have developed this idea in the following framework:

1. We all feel a longing for something more, and this longing is meant to be filled by God.

2. Idolatry in the Hebrew Scriptures describes the worship of Baal, Asherah, or other deities. In our lives, the same sin can (and does) occur; though most of us are technically monotheistic; we're constantly putting things above God in the practical way we live, filling our need with things which are not meant to satisfy it.

3. Money, sex, power, success, fame, approval, things, comfort, experiences, other people, and a host of other things promise us self-esteem, validation, and pleasure; these things ultimately cannot deliver and, more so, our enjoyment of them is compromised when we put pressure on them to act as gods.

4. Refocusing on Jesus as the source of validation will push out our unhealthy attachment to idols, and it will allow us to live less destructive, more satisfied/joyous lives.

Others have pushed the point to the absurd. Implicit in this view of idolatry lies the assumption that God will be reliably present in bible reading, prayer, meditation, good deeds, etc; and He will be reliably absent in selfishness, power, pursuit of fame, etc. Pinning God down beneath the human gaze of a book (such as the Bible), virtuous behavior, good works, quiet time, and so forth, may be an attempt to make the Lord manageable and perceivable, visible and measurable. **Idolatry then is reducing God to a deity that can be manipulated.** This sounds like the beginning of idolatry. We want to take avenues of God's presence and make them tangible.

This whole discussion becomes confusing when what are thought of as "the means of grace" or "spiritual disciplines" can be portrayed as "idols." It reminds me of the diabolical accusation, "You're just generous toward others because it makes you feel good," so that generosity becomes selfishness. Really, as teachers of the things of God, we need to stop confusing people. I have no doubt that such thinking pleases the devil, but it cannot be pleasing to God.

Another workable definition for modern-day **idolatry is worshiping the creature rather than the creator.** Under this definition is our unhealthy attention given to superstars in music, theater or politics. Also, under this heading would be our obsession with anything we love too dearly, which has our undivided attention and affection, the thing rather than the creator of the thing.

Some say that modern idolatry often has self-worship at its core. This manifests in all forms of selfishness, self love and self absorption. The extreme is the classic sociopath who sees himself as the center of the universe while having no empathy for those around him. Charles Manson states that he is his own god. O.J. Simpson still thinks of Nicole from time to time and becomes angry at her because she is not there to help raise their daughter. Say what?!

Others have defined it in the broad sense of any earthly lust, the lust of the flesh, lust of the eyes and the boastful pride of life (1 John 2:16).

We know that the Bible tells us to put God first and that we will do this in the spirit of true worship of God. All of life becomes worship in this sense and **anything detracting from true worship becomes idolatry.**

But above all pursue his kingdom and righteousness, and all these things [the necessities of life] will be given to you as well (Matt 6:33).

Do not accumulate for yourselves treasures on earth, where moth and rust destroy and where thieves break in

137

and steal. But accumulate for yourselves treasure in heaven where moth and rust do not destroy, and thieves do not break in and steal. For where your treasure is, there you heart will be also. The eye is the lamp of the body. If then your eye is healthy, your whole body will be full of light. But if your eye is diseased, your whole body will be full of darkness. If then the light in you is darkness, how great is the darkness! No one can serve two masters, for either he will hate the one and love the other, or he will be devoted to the one and despise the other. You cannot serve both God and mammon" (Matt 6:19-21).

Whoever loves father or mother more than me is not worthy of Me, and whoever loves son or daughter more than me is not worthy of Me. And whoever does not take up his cross and follow Me is not worthy of me. Whoever finds his life will lose it, and whoever loses his life because of Me will find it (Matt 10:37-39).

Keep thinking about things above, not things on the earth, for you have died and your life is hidden with Christ in God. When Christ (who is your life) appears, then you too will be revealed in glory with Him (Col 3:2-3).

John Wesley interpreted idolatry as the underlying sin beneath all others. The Wesleyan-Holiness movement made idolatry the primary problem overcome by entire sanctification, and the key detractor from the life of holiness. The Old Testament, like the New, calls persons to a single eye, an undivided heart, and worship of God alone. This prohibition against idolatry comes out of Israel's covenantal relationship with the Holy One.[65]

As believers in Jesus Christ, our worldview is to see Him "before all things and all things held together in Him." If religion is the attempt to live in harmony with the power one believes is controlling the universe, then, for the Christian, that is Jesus (Col 1:15-18). But, we must distinguish ourselves through total commitment to Him, trust in Him, and devotion toward Him. It is not enough just to "live in harmony" with Him. It is not enough for us to say, "I know there is a god; I don't bother him, and He doesn't bother me," as one man said to us. Christianity is radical, not lukewarm. It must of necessity lead to deeper worship in spirit and in truth. Only then can we completely avoid the spirit of idolatry. We must know the God whom we worship, and worship no other.

CHAPTER 12
SECULAR HUMANISM AND CULTURAL CAPTIVITY

Christianity is not a series of truths in the plural, but rather truth spelled with a capital "T." Biblical Christianity is Truth concerning total reality – and the intellectual holding of that total Truth and then living in the light of that Truth. (Francis Schaeffer, Address at the University of Notre Dame, April 1981)

Secular Humanism is an outlook or philosophy that advocates human rather than religious values. Confucianism seems to suggest a similar worldview. Along with atheism, agnosticism, skepticism, Marxism and existentialism, secular humanism may be labeled a "secular religion." This worldview can easily co-exist with compromised religion including so-called Christianity. In truth it is antithetical to Christianity, because the Christian must deny himself, take up his cross daily and follow Jesus Christ. He will base his worldview on Jesus and the Scriptures. The Christian will not lean on his own understanding, but in all his ways acknowledge God the Father. <u>While secular humanism begins and ends with man, the Bible starts and ends with God.</u>

God, who made the world and everything in it, since He is Lord of heaven and earth, does not dwell in temples made with hands. Nor is He worshiped with men's hands, as though He needed anything, since He gives to all life, breath, and all things. And He has made from one blood every nation of men to dwell on all the face of the earth, and has determined their preappointed times and the boundaries of their dwellings, so that they should seek the Lord, in the hope that they might grope for Him and find Him, though He is not far from each one of us; for in Him we live and move and have our being, as also some of your own poets have said, 'For we are also His offspring' (Acts 17:24-28).

Humanism itself is the overall attitude that human beings are of special value; their aspirations, their thoughts, their yearnings are significant. There is as well an emphasis on the value of the individual person. [66]

As evangelical Christians <u>we believe that our reasoning ability was given to us by God in whose image we were created</u>, and that responsible use of our reasoning ability to understand the world around us can lead us to sound evidence for the existence of God. Secular humanism rejects the idea of life after death, dogmatically asserting that it is impossible to prove. On the contrary, <u>the resurrection of Jesus Christ from the dead is a fact of history</u>, verifiable by standard historical tests. His resurrection becomes the seal and the hope of every Christian.

For I know that my Redeemer lives, And He shall stand at last on the earth; And after my skin is destroyed, this I know, That in my flesh I shall see God, Whom I shall see for myself, And my eyes shall behold, and not another. How my heart yearns within me! (Job 19:25-27)

But I do not want you to be ignorant, brethren, concerning those who have fallen asleep, lest you sorrow as others who have no hope. For if we believe that Jesus died and rose again, even so God will bring with Him those who sleep in Jesus. For this we say to you by the word of the

Lord, that we who are alive and remain until the coming of the Lord will by no means precede those who are asleep. For the Lord Himself will descend from heaven with a shout, with the voice of an archangel, and with the trumpet of God. And the dead in Christ will rise first. Then we who are alive and remain shall be caught up together with them in the clouds to meet the Lord in the air. And thus we shall always be with the Lord. Therefore comfort one another with these words (1Thes 4:13-18).

For we know that if our earthly house, this tent, is destroyed, we have a building from God, a house not made with hands, eternal in the heavens. For in this we groan, earnestly desiring to be clothed with our habitation which is from heaven, if indeed, having been clothed, we shall not be found naked. For we who are in this tent groan, being burdened, not because we want to be unclothed, but further clothed, that mortality may be swallowed up by life. Now He who has prepared us for this very thing is God, who also has given us the Spirit as a guarantee. So we are always confident, knowing that while we are at home in the body we are absent from the Lord. For we walk by faith, not by sight (2 Cor 4:1-7).

But now Christ is risen from the dead, and has become the firstfruits of those who have fallen asleep. For since by man came death, by Man also came the resurrection of the dead. For as in Adam all die, even so in Christ all shall be made alive. But each one in his own order: Christ the firstfruits, afterward those who are Christ's at His coming. Then comes the end, when He delivers the kingdom to God the Father, when He puts an end to all rule and all authority and power. For He must reign till He has put all enemies under His feet. The last enemy [that] will be *destroyed is death. For "He has put all things under His feet." But when He says "all things are put under Him," it is evident that He who put all things under Him is excepted. Now when all things are made subject to Him, then the Son Himself will also be subject to Him who put all things under Him, that God may be all in all. ...But someone will say, "How are the dead raised up? And with what body do they come?" Foolish one, what you sow is not made alive unless it dies. And what you sow, you do not sow that body that shall be, but mere grain--perhaps wheat or some other grain. But God gives it a body as He pleases, and to each seed its own body. All flesh is not the same flesh, but there is one kind of flesh of men, another flesh of animals, another of fish, and another of birds. There are also celestial bodies and terrestrial bodies; but the glory of the celestial is one, and the [glory] of the terrestrial is another. There is one glory of the sun, another glory of the moon, and another glory of the stars; for one star differs from another star in glory. So also is the resurrection of the dead. The body is sown in corruption, it is raised in incorruption. It is sown in dishonor, it is raised in glory. It is sown in weakness, it is raised in power. It is sown a natural body, it is raised a spiritual body. There is a natural body, and there is a spiritual body. And so it is written, "The first man Adam became a living being." The last Adam became a life-giving spirit. However, the spiritual is not first, but the natural, and afterward the spiritual. The first man was of the earth, made of dust; the second Man is the Lord from heaven. As was the man of dust, so also are those who are made of dust; and as is the heavenly Man, so also are those who are heavenly. And as we have borne the image of the man of dust, we shall also bear the image of the heavenly Man. Now this I say, brethren, that flesh and blood cannot inherit the kingdom of God; nor does corruption inherit incorruption. Behold, I tell you a mystery: We shall not all sleep, but we shall all be changed--in a moment, in the twinkling of an eye, at the last trumpet. For the trumpet will sound, and the dead will be raised incorruptible, and we shall be changed. For this corruptible must put on incorruption, and this mortal must put on immortality. So when this corruptible has put on incorruption, and this mortal has put on immortality, then shall be brought to pass the saying that is written: "Death is swallowed up in victory." (2 Cor 15:20-28, 35-54)*

Satan in his worldview strategy would not only discredit the historical aspect of our hope in everlasting life, but he would dismantle the foundations of our morality as merely opinion. With secularism the determination of good or evil is always situational and dependent upon a group of like-minded individuals. <u>Christianity asserts that there is absolute good and evil. Our moral attributes are patterned after the nature and attributes of our creator, God.</u> Similarly, humanism attempts to discover solutions to the problems of mankind through science and technology, reasoning that rules of order for forming better societies will arise out of this study. Christians are not adverse to science and technology, knowing that <u>the Christian God who created the world determined the laws and functions which are discovered by Science</u>.

For by Him all things were created that are in heaven and that are on earth, visible and invisible, whether thrones or dominions or principalities or powers. All things were created through Him and for Him. And He is before all things, and in Him all things consist (Col 1:16-17).

Finally, secular humanism states that we must learn to live openly together or we will perish together. That is in total agreement with scripture. However, the Bible states that because man Is basically self-centered and sinful, he will never be able to live peaceably with his fellow man on his own initiative. It takes the super-natural intervention of God to transform individuals into selfless, caring, loving people who really will sacrifice their own desires for the sake of their fellow men. Universal peace will come only with the intervention of Almighty God.

Knowing this first: that scoffers will come in the last days, walking according to their own lusts, and saying, "Where is the promise of His coming? For since the fathers fell asleep, all things continue as they were from the beginning of creation." For this they willfully forget: that by the word of God the heavens were of old, and the earth standing out of water and in the water, by which the world that then existed perished, being flooded with water. But the heavens and the earth which are now preserved by the same word, are reserved for fire until the day of judgment and perdition of ungodly men. But, beloved, do not forget this one thing, that with the Lord one day is as a thousand years, and a thousand years as one day. The Lord is not slack concerning His promise, as some count slackness, but is longsuffering toward us, not willing that any should perish but that all should come to repentance. But the day of the Lord will come as a thief in the night, in which the heavens will pass away with a great noise, and the elements will melt with fervent heat; both the earth and the works that are in it will be burned up. Therefore, since all these things will be dissolved, what manner of persons ought you to be in holy conduct and godliness, looking for and hastening the coming of the day of God, because of which the heavens will be dissolved, being on fire, and the elements will melt with fervent heat? Nevertheless we, according to His promise, look for new heavens and a new earth in which righteousness dwells. Therefore, beloved, looking forward to these things, be diligent to be found by Him in peace, without spot and blameless (2 Pet 3:3-14).

Cultural Captivity

Now why, since there is a distinct Christian worldview, do Christians think that their faith in Jesus is private business? Why do so many of us live two lives, one for church and family, another for business and social life outside the church.   There is a life for "personal evangelism" and another life for politics and civic responsibility.   After reading Charles Colson and Nancy Pearcey's *Now How Shall We Live*, with its positive message that Christians can make a real impact on their world beyond one-to-one evangelism, that they can affect change in institutions and societies, I began looking for other books written by Nancy Pearcey. I discovered *Total Truth* whose theme is "liberating Christianity from its cultural captivity." She explains there how the Christian worldview incorporates all that we think, say and do in life, that its tenants and purpose are all-embracing and that the typical Christian has too small of a worldview. Put another way, Christians have been satisfied to lead two lives. This reminds one of the ancient Jews who adopted foreign idols like Baal into their cultural lifestyle while holding on to their belief in the Torah when convenient. This compartmentalization of worldviews, this duality brings confusion to say the least. In fact, it brings the anger of God as revealed in the Bible. It was not acceptable then, and it is not acceptable today. This pretense results in the fracturing and fragmenting of our lives with our faith firmly locked into the private realm of church and family, where it rarely has a chance to inform our life and work in the public realm. Evangelicals have typically accented personal piety and individual salvation, leaving men to their own devices to interpret the world around them.[67] This is none other than the "double-minded man, unstable in all his ways" (James 1:8).

Our children are not being taught the Christian worldview unless it is lived in the home. Even in many Christian schools, the typical strategy is to inject a few narrowly defined "religious" elements into the classroom, like prayer and Bible memorization – and then teach exactly the same things as the secular schools. The curriculum merely spreads a layer of spiritual devotion over the subject matter like icing on a cake, while the content itself stays the same. The same pattern holds all the way up to the highest academic levels. Even Christian professors, let alone secular, have conceded the theories, concepts and other subject matter that are conventional in the respective disciplines to secularists as long as Christians are allowed to hold bible studies and prayer meetings.[68]

This fracture becomes a type of idolatry for the Christian. Humans are inherently religious beings, created to be in relationship with God – and if they reject God, they don't stop being religious; they simply find some other ultimate principle upon which to base their lives.[69] What is the antidote to the secular/sacred divide? We must begin by being utterly convinced that there is a biblical perspective on everything – not just on spiritual matters. All truth must begin with God. Nothing exists apart from His will; nothing falls outside the scope of the central turning points in biblical history: Creation, Fall, and Redemption. These are the great themes for all of life. For what purpose has God created us and sustained us? What has been the effect of the fall from His grace and into sin?   And, what was accomplished in His redemption for mankind. What does He intend for us now? This "Biblical Toolbox" [70] will enable us to break out of the grid of double-mindedness which confines us and stunts our growth, both spiritual and intellectual. When one dares to break out of the secular-humanist presumption that Christianity stunts open-mindedness and connection to the real world, long held assumptions are overcome by science itself that show the success of the Christian worldview in philosophy, the healing of mind and body and the success of "compassionate conservatism." If Christianity really is true, then it will yield a better approach in every discipline.[71]

A Balanced Christian Worldview

Nancy Pearcey gives us wonderful insight into maintaining a balanced Christian worldview with her rubric of both presenting the gospel and defending the faith in terms of the Christian worldview. The explanation must begin with creation, the reality that what God created was very good, that man was first created in the image of God, and furthermore, that all God created is good. Only then can the tragedy of the fall be understood; only then can the impact of sin be appreciated. Finally, and in this order, redemption can be grasped as both necessary and sufficient to remedy the sin. Redemption can be understood as the return to what God so perfectly created in the first place. When approached out of order and out of balance ones worldview is adversely affected. If one begins with the fall, the message of salvation is rendered incoherent.

Today, as we address the biblically illiterate Americans of the twenty-first century, we need to follow Paul's model, building a case from Creation before expecting people to understand the message of sin and salvation. We need to practice "pre-evangelism," using apologetics to defend basic concepts of who God is, who we are, and what we owe Him, before presenting the gospel message.[72]

It may be a bit of academic elitism to suppose that we can approach everyone in this manner. We must realize that God is reaching out to each human being on every level. He is making his creation evident to them by general revelation before the gospel is preached regarding sin. Nevertheless, Nancy Pearsey's rubric of Creation, Fall and Redemption presents a wonderful outline for both evangelism and defense of the faith. That is because it describes a balanced Christian worldview which disallows non-biblical principles in the argument.

The promise of Christianity is the joy and power of an integrated life, transformed on every level by the Holy Spirit, so that our whole being participates in the great drama of God's plan of redemption.[73]

Finally, each Christian must come to grips with how his Christian worldview commands his everyday activity. Whether spectator or testimony, we all are looking for genuine people who are morally and intellectually honest, who refuse to be involved in deception for any reason. I am willing to put myself to the ultimate test. What are the consequences of giving up everything for the cause of Christ? What are the ramifications of selling all that I have for the pearl of great price? Am I going to become a believer only to live and behave exactly like a non-believer? What is it to be so grafted in the vine of Christ that I should bear good fruit? What is it that I should count all things but loss for the sake of knowing Christ and the power of His resurrection, the fellowship of His sufferings, and the hope of life eternal? If living out ones worldview can answer these questions, they will surely be made clearer as time goes by. *"For now we see through a glass darkly; but then face to face: now I know in part; but then shall I know even as also I am known"* (1 Cor 13:12). Until that day I will be satisfied that through His Word God has provided the most comprehensive explanation and pattern for living and understanding. This is my worldview. And it is uncompromisingly Christian.

CHAPTER 13

CHRISTIAN ORTHODOXY AND HERESY

If Worldview is guided by Scriptural doctrine, one must guard against false doctrine in order to have a consistent worldview. Heresy obviously depends upon orthodoxy. Roger Olsen points out that if Christianity is compatible with anything and everything, it is nothing.[74] The upshot of the belief that all beliefs are equally true is at best "folk religion." Such is the result of relativism. Counterfeits have been around for a very long time. Paul wrote of them in his letters. Some beliefs are virtually held as essential by all Christians and are essential to authentic Christianity. These have been traditionally expressed as creed, e.g. *The* Nicene Creed, 325 AD, still used today:

> *I believe in one God the Father Almighty,*
> *Maker of heaven and earth,*
> *and of all things visible and invisible;*
> *And in one Lord Jesus Christ,*
> *the only-begotten of His Father before all worlds,*
> *God of God, Light of Light,*
> *very God of vey God,*
> *begotten, not made,*
> *being of one substance with the Father,*
> *by whom all things were made;*
> *who for us and for our salvation came down from*
> *heaven,*
> *and was incarnate by the Holy Spirit of the Virgin Mary,*
> *and was made man,*
> *and crucified also for us under Pontius Pilate;*

He suffered and was buried,
and the third day He rose again according to the
Scriptures,
and ascended into heaven,
and sitteth on the right hand of the Father;
and He shall come again with glory to judge both the
living and the dead;
whose kingdom shall have no end.
And I believe in the Holy Spirit,
the Lord and Giver of life,
who proceedeth from the Father and the Son,
who with the Father and the Son together is worshiped
and glorified;
who spoke by the prophets.
And I believe in one universal and apostolic church;
I acknowledge one baptism for the remission of sins;
and I look for the resurrection of the dead,
and the life of the world to come.
Amen.

This and *The Apostles Creed* are shared by almost any Christian denomination and are therefore orthodox.

Heresy, on the other hand, usually arises when sincere men thought they had discovered some truth the rest of the church was missing. In most cases, the reasoning had to do with Jesus Christ and salvation (Christology and Soteriology). The heresies condemned as such by early Christians, before and after Constantine, were judged then and have been judged by most Christians ever since to change the truth about Jesus Christ or salvation into something else – different gospels. Apostolic authority and orthodox Christianity have rejected "any other gospel" as directed by Scripture:

But even if we, or an angel from heaven, were to preach any other gospel *unto you than that which we have* preached *unto you, let him be* anathema (Gal 1:8).

Loathing and denouncing that which does not fit orthodox Christianity is necessary to avoid half-truths, confusion and inconsistency with Scripture. That is why orthodoxy, or "mere Christianity" as C.S. Lewis called it, is necessary to a Christian worldview.

These are not mere doctrinal differences, such as how and when one should be baptized or whether speaking in tongues is an esoteric Holy Spirit language. It is not whether we should celebrate the Sabbath only on Saturday or whether the times expressed in the Bible are divided into dispensations or covenants. Heresies are contradictions to the gospel which should be identified as false teachings.

CHAPTER 14
THE UNIQUELY CHRISTIAN WORLDVIEW

Hugely entertaining is the 2nd Century letter of Mathetes to Diognetus (c.130-200 A.D.). Diognetus was a tutor of the emperor Marcus Aurelius. This letter is an apologetic for the Christians, an earnest description from a Christian disciple. The following is a translation of Chapter 5: [75]

Christians are not distinguished from other men by country, language, nor by the customs which they observe. They do not inhabit cities of their own, use a particular way of speaking, nor lead a life marked out by any curiosity. The course of conduct they follow has not been devised by the speculation and deliberation of inquisitive men. They do not, like some, proclaim themselves the advocates of merely human doctrines. Instead, they inhabit both Greek and barbarian cities, however things have fallen to each of them. And it is while following the customs of the natives in clothing, food, and the rest of ordinary life that they display to us their wonderful and admittedly striking way of life. They live in their own countries, but they do so as those who are just passing through. As citizens they participate in everything with others, yet they endure everything as if they were foreigners. Every foreign land is like their homeland to them, and every land of their birth is like a land of strangers. They marry, like everyone else, and they have children, but they do not destroy their offspring. They share a common table, but not a common bed. They exist in the flesh, but they do not live by the flesh. They pass

their days on earth, but they are citizens of heaven. They
obey the prescribed laws, all the while surpassing the laws
by their lives. They love all men and are persecuted by all.
They are unknown and condemned. They are put to death
and restored to life. They are poor, yet make many rich.
They lack everything, yet they overflow in everything.
They are dishonored, and yet in their very dishonor they
are glorified; they are spoken ill of and yet are justified;
they are reviled but bless; they are insulted and repay the
insult with honor; they do good, yet are punished as
evildoers; when punished, they rejoice as if raised from the
dead. They are assailed by the Jews as barbarians; they are
persecuted by the Greeks; yet those who hate them are
unable to give any reason for their hatred.

This testimony, merely a century after the resurrection, from a Christian disciple quotes no scripture and does not mention the name of Jesus. But it gives some insight into what it must have been like to be a 2nd Century Christian. Eighteen centuries have passed since then, but we recognize these words from an early believer as a description of contemporary Christians.

With two millennia of reflection on the Gospel and writings we can make these extrapolations:

- Christianity is based in verifiable history.

We did not follow cleverly invented stories when we told
you about the power and coming of our Lord Jesus Christ,
but we were eyewitnesses of his majesty (2 Peter 1:16).

What we have seen with our eyes, what we have beheld
and our hands handled...we bear witness and proclaim to
you (1 John 1:1-3).

- Secondly, all other religions exhort man to reach up to God and grasp hold of Him through their own efforts. <u>Christianity is the only religion where God reaches down to man</u>.

- Thirdly, other religions are systems of do's and don'ts to appease their god; whereas <u>Christianity is a relationship with God</u>.

- Also, Christianity looks to God's Word, <u>the Bible, as the singular source of Truth</u>.

- Finally, <u>Christianity is based upon</u> truly the most amazing event in all of human history—<u>the resurrection</u>.

In their discussion of worldviews which thoroughly would include *theism, atheism, pantheism, panentheism, deism, polytheism* and *finite godism*, Norman Geisler and Peter Bocchino make clear that all have permeated our culture and existence.

"Where then are we today," asks James Sire. In terms of possible worldviews, our options are numerous, although we have found ways to limit them. All but theism have serious flaws. If my argument has been correct, none of them - deism, naturalism, existentialism, Eastern pantheistic monism or New Age philosophy, nor the postmodern perspective – can adequately account for the possibility of genuine knowledge, the facticity of the universe or the existence of ethical distinctions. Each in its own way ends in some form of nihilism.[76] We, however, have chosen ultimately to receive God's truth in plain view, and to trust what has been revealed to us.

...because what may be known of God is manifest in them, for God has shown it to them. For since the creation of the world his invisible attributes are clearly seen, being understood by the things that are made, even His eternal power and Godhead, so that they are without excuse (Rom 1:19-20)

From a Christian *worldview* we see that God will hold us each and all accountable for what has been revealed about Himself through general revelation. But mankind is not limited to general revelation because He has also revealed Himself in the special revelation of Israel and, ultimately, in God's Son, Jesus Christ.

[God] has in these last days spoken to us by His Son, whom He has appointed heir of all things, through whom also He made the worlds; who being the brightness of His glory and the express image of His person, and upholding all things by the word of His power, when He had by Himself purged our sins, sat down at the right hand of the Majesty on high (Heb 1:2-3).

While the most fundamental dissension between worldviews is based on the existence and nature of God, there are several more distinctions that should be made. Geisler and Bocchino, limiting themselves to just three worldviews: atheism, pantheism and theism, provide this comparison with that of Christianity: [77]

a. What do Atheists Believe?

- GOD – He does not exist; only the universe exists.

- UNIVERSE – It is eternal; or it randomly came to be.
- HUMANITY (origin) – We have evolved, are made of molecules, and are not immoral.
- HUMANITY (destiny) – We have no eternal destiny and will be annihilated.
- EVIL (origin) – It is real, caused by human ignorance.
- EVIL (destiny) – It can be defeated by man through education.
- ETHICS (basis) – They are created by, and grounded in, humanity.
- ETHICS (nature) – They are relative, determined by the situation.

b. What do Pantheists Believe?

1. GOD – He is one, infinite, usually impersonal; he is the universe.
2. UNIVERSE – It is an illusion, a manifestation of God, who alone is real.
3. HUMANITY (origin) – The human's true self (atman) is God (Brahman).
4. HUMANITY (destiny) – Our destiny is determined by karma/cycles of life.
5. EVIL (origin) – It is an illusion, caused by errors of the mind.
6. EVIL (destiny) – It will be reabsorbed by God.
7. ETHICS (basis) – They are grounded in lower manifestations of God.
8. ETHICS (nature) – They are relative, transcending the illusion of good and evil.

c. What do Theists Believe?

- GOD – He is one, personal, moral, infinite in all His attributes.
- UNIVERSE – It is finite, created by an infinite God.
- HUMANITY (origin) – We are immortal, created and sustained by God.
- HUMANITY (destiny) – By choice we'll be either eternally with or separated from God.
- EVIL (origin) – It is privation or imperfection caused by choice.
- EVIL (destiny) – It will be ultimately defeated by God.
- ETHICS (basis) – They are grounded in the nature of God.
- ETHICS (nature) – They are absolute, objective, and prescriptive.

When these worldviews are mixed into a potpourri of beliefs and aphorisms, they yield worldview confusion. This book has endeavored to offer clarification for the Christian worldview to avoid this confusion.

For God is not the author of confusion but of peace, as in all the churches of the saints (1 Cor 14:33).

As such, it is important to ask the right questions and to determine what we do not believe as well as what we believe. Here is the bottom line: <u>The object of Christianity is not so much to be religious as to know God through Jesus Christ</u>. We are separated from His fellowship when there is sin in our lives. The relationship is restored only through the gift given by the blood of Jesus. God made Him who knew no sin to become sin for us (2 Cor 5:21). One could therefore argue that Christianity is not a religion at all.

How shall we escape if we neglect so great a salvation? (Heb 2:3)

It follows that we would respond with all that is within us in thanksgiving and worship to serve our God with all of our heart, mind and strength and to love our neighbor as ourselves. It follows that we should want to become Christ-like in all that we are and do. And, it follows that we should want to share the good news of Jesus Christ, the hope of resurrection within us and the warning of His ultimate return and judgment to all with whom we come into contact.

A SELECT BIBLIOGRAPHY

Ankersmit, F.R. *History and Tropology: The Rise and Fall of Metaphor.* Oakland, CA: Univ. of California Press, 1994.

Bacon, Francis. "Novum Organum" from *The Works*, 3 vols. Philadelphia: Parry & MacMillan, 1854.

Barzun, Jacques and Henry F. Graff. *The Modern Researcher.* Rev. ed. New York: Harcourt, Brace & World, Inc., 1970.

Byl, John. *The Divine Challenge: On Matter, Mind, Math & Meaning.* Carlisle, PA: The Banner of Truth Trust, 2004.

Colingwood, R.G. *The Idea of history*, 1936. New York: Oxford Univ. Press edition, reprint 1994.

Colson, Charles, and Nancy Pearcey. *How Now Shall We Live?* Wheaton, IL: Tyndale House Publishers, Inc., 1999.

Geisler, Norman L. "Historical Apologetics," *Baker Encyclopedia of Christian Apologetics*, Grand Rapids: Baker Academic, 1999.

Geisler, Norman L. "History, Objectivity of," *Baker Encyclopedia of Christian Apologetics*, Grand Rapids: Baker Academic, 1999.

Geisler, Norman. "Worldview," *Baker Encyclopedia of Christian Apologetics.* Grand Rapids, MI: Baker Academic, 1999.

Geisler, Norman and Peter Bocchino. *Unshakable Foundations: Contemporary Answers to Crucial Questions about the Christian Faith*. Bloomington, MN: Bethany House Publishers, 2001.

Gruber, David. *The Church and the Jews: The Biblical Relationship*. Springfield, MO: General Council of the Assemblies of God, Intercultural Ministries, 1991.

Henry, Patrick. "Give Me Liberty or Give Me Death" (1816) speech (see www.history.org/ almanac/life/politics/ giveme.cfm).

Hume, David. *"An Enquiry Concerning Human Understanding"* (1748), Sect. VIII, Part 1. L.A. Selby-Bigge edition. Oxford at the Clarendon Press, 1972.

Kaiser, Walter C. *The Promise-Plan of God: A Biblical Theology of the Old and New Testaments*. Grand Rapids, MI: Zondervan, 2008.

Lapid, Pinchas. Israelis, Jews and Jesus. Garden City, NJ: Doubleday and Co., 1979.

Leclerk, Diane. *Discovering Christian Holiness: The Heart of Wesleyan-Holiness Theology*. Kansas City, MO: The Beacon Hill Press, 2010.

Lemon, M.C. *Philosophy of History: A Guide for Students*. London and New York: Routledge, 2003.

Lindsey, Hal. *The Everlasting Hatred: The Roots of Jihad*. Washington D.C.: WND Books, 2011.

Macchiavelli, Niccolo. *The Prince*, (1532) (see www.constitution.org/mac/prince18.htm.)

MacArthur, John, ed. *Think Biblically!: Recovering a Christian Worldview*. Wheaton, IL: Crossway Books, 2003.

MacArthur, John. *Right Thinking in a World gone Wrong: A Biblical Response to Today's Most Controversial Issues*. Eugene, OR: Harvest House Publishers, 2009.

McCumber, W.E. *Was It Not I? And Other Questions God Asks*. Kansas City, MO: Beacon Hill Press, 1994.

McDowell, Josh and Don Stewart. *Handbook of Today's Religions*. San Bernardino, CA: Here's Life Publishers, Inc., 1983.

Montgomery, John Warwick. *Tractatus Logico Theologicus*. Bonn, Germany: Verlag für Kultur und Wissenschaft, 2002.

Nietzsche, Friedrich. *On the Advantage and Disadvantage of History for Life*, 1874, transl. by Peter Preuss. Indianapolis: Hackett Publishing Co., 1980.

Ostler, Nicholas. *Empires of the Word, a Language History of the World*. Great Britain: Harper Collins Publishers, 2005.

Palmer, Michael D., ed. *Elements of a Christian Worldview*. Springfield, MO: Logion Press, 1998.

Pearcey, Nancy R. *Total Truth: Liberating Christianity from Its Cultural Captivity*. Wheaton,IL: Crossway Books, 2004.

Penrose, Roger. *Shadows of the Mind: A Search for the Missing Science of Consciousness.* Oxford University Press, 1994.

Rousseau, Jean Jacques. *The Social Contract* (1762), Book II, part 7, "The Legislator" (see www.constitution.org/jjr/ocon_02.htm).

Samdahl, Don. http://doctrine.org/the-olive-tree/. Updated April 16, 2012.

Schaeffer, Francis. *How Should We Then Live? The Rise and Decline of Western Thought and Culture.* Wheaton, IL: Crossway, 1976.

Schaeffer, Francis. *Trilogy: The God Who is There; Escape from Reason; He is There and He is Not Silent.* Wheaton, IL: Crossway Books, 1990.

Schopenhaur, Arthur. *The World as Will and Representation*, Vol. 1. Mineola, NY: Dover Publications Inc., 1969.

Shelley, Bruce L. *Church History in Plain Language*, Updated 2nd Edition. Nashville: Thomas Nelson Publishers, 1995.

Sire, James W. *The Universe Next Door*, 5th ed. Downers Grove, IL: Intervarsity Press, 2009.

Sorokin, Pitirim. *Social & Cultural Dynamics*, 1975 ed. Reprint, Transaction Publishers, 1985.

Sproul, R.C. *The Consequences of Ideas.* Wheaton, IL: Crossway Books, 2000.

Stanford, Michael. *An Introduction to the Philosophy of History.* Oxford, UK: Blackwell Publishers, 1998.

Tillich, Paul. *A History of Christian Thought.* New York: Simon and Schuster, 1967.

Tucker, Ruth A. *Another Gospel: Alternative Religions and the New Age Movement.* Grand Rapids, MI: Zondervan Publishing House, 1989.

White, Hayden. *Metahistory: The Historical Imagination in Nineteenth Century Europe.* Baltimore, MA: Johns Hopkins Univ. Press, 1975.

Zacharias, Ravi. *Jesus Among Other Gods: The Absolute Claims of the Christian Message.* Nashville: Word Publishing, 2000.

NOTES
for A Uniquely Christian Worldview

Chap 1

1. Ravi Zacharias. *Jesus Among Other Gods.* (Nashville: Word Publishing, 2000), p. 3-4.

2. Appendix B provides a glossary for the purpose of clarity especially for those who are not accustomed to some of the terms used in the discussion of the philosophy of history, worldviews, comparative religions and biblical interpretation. Words in the glossary are shown in italics in the body of this writing.

3. James W. Sire. *The Universe Next Door.* 5th ed. (Downers Grove, IL: Intervarsity Press, 2009), p. 283.

4. Billie Davis. "A Perspective of Human Nature," in *Elements of a Christian Worldview*, ed. by Michael D. Palmer. (Springfield, MO: Logion Press, 1998), 204-205

5. John Byle. *The Divine Challenge: On Matter, Mind, Math & Meaning.* Chap 10, "The Christian Worldview" (Carlisle, PA: The Banner of Truth Trust, 2004).

6. Edar R. Lee, "The Role of the Bible in Shaping a Christian Worldview," in <u>Elements of a Christian Worldview</u>, ed. by Michael D. Palmer. (Springfield, MO: Logion Press, 1998), p.80.

7. Byle. op.cit. p.194-195.

8. Byle, op.cit., pp. 280-281.

9. Byle, op.cit., pp.290-291.

10. Del Tackett. *"What's a Christian Worldview?* http://www.focusonthefamily.com/faith/christian worldview/whats_a_christian_worldview.aspx

11. James Sire. The Universe Next Door, 5th ed. (Donners Grove, IL: Intervarsity Press, 2004, p. 97

12. R.C. Sproul. *The Consequences of Ideas* (Wheaton, IL: Crossway Books, 2000), pp.200-202.

13. Ibid. p.203

Chap 2

14. Arthur F. Holmes. *All Truth is God's Truth* (Downers Grove, IL: IVP, 1977).

15. Taylor B. Jones "Why a Scriptural View of Science," in Think Biblically! John MacArthur, ed. (Wheaton, IL: Crossway Books, 2003), p. 233.

16. Del Tackett. *"What's Your View of the World,"* www.focuson thefamily.com/faith/christianworldview /whats_a_christian_worldview.aspx

17. For purposes of George Barna's research, a biblical worldview was defined as believing that absolute moral truths exist; that such truth is defined by the Bible; and firm belief in six specific religious views. Those views were that Jesus Christ lived a sinless life; God is the all-powerful and all-knowing Creator of the universe and He stills rules it today; salvation is a gift from God and cannot be earned; Satan is real; Christians have a responsibility to share their faith in Christ with other people; and the Bible is accurate in all of its teachings. In Barna Research Group studies, born again Christians are not defined on the basis of characterizing themselves as "born again" but based upon their answers to two questions. The first is "have you ever made a personal commitment to Jesus Christ that is still important in your life today?" If the respondent says "yes," then they are asked a follow-up question about life after death. One of the seven perspectives a respondent may choose is "when I die, I will go to Heaven because I have confessed my sins and have accepted Jesus Christ as my savior." Individuals who answer "yes" to the first question and select this statement as their belief about their own salvation are then categorized as "born again."

18. Tracy F. Munsil. *"What's Your Worldview?"* http://www.focus
onthefamily.com/faith/christian_worldview
/whats_a_christian_ worldview
/whats_your_worldview.aspx

Chap 3

19. John Warwick Montgomery. *Tractatus Logico Theologicus.*
(Bonn, Germany: Verlag für Kultur und Wissenschaft,
2002), pp.158-159.

20. Montgomery. Op.cit., p.84

21.Jacques Barzun & Henry F. Graff. *The Modern Researcher* (New
York: Harcourt, Brace & World, Inc., 1970), pp.58-62.

22. Byle, op.cit., pp.280-281.

23. Michael Stanford. *An Introduction to the Philosophy of History.*
(Oxford, UK: Blackwell Publishers, 1998), pp.76-77.

Chap 4

24. Stanford. op.cit., p.196.

25. Billie Davis. op. cit., p. 204.

26. Nicholas Ostler. *Empires of the Word: A Language History of
the World.* (Great Britain: Harper Collins Publishers, 2005),
p. xix.

27. Clyde P. Greer. op.cit., p. 262.

28. Paul Tillich. *A History of Christian Thought.* (New York:
Simon and Schuster, 1967), pp.34-35.

29. Bruce Shelley. *Church history in Plain Language*, updated 2nd
ed. (Nashville: Thomas Nelson Publishers, 1995), p.192.

30. Niccolo Machiavelli. *The Prince*, Chapter 18 "Concerning the
Way in Which Princes Should keep Faith," (see
www.constitution.org/mac/prince18.htm).

31. Francis Bacon. "Novum Organum" from *The Works*, 3 vols. (Philadelphia: Parry & MacMillan, 1854), 3:345-360.

32. Jean Jacques Rousseau. *The Social Contract*, Book II, part 7, "The Legislator" (see www.constitution.org /jjr/socon_02.htm).

33. Patrick Henry, 1775, in his *"Give Me Liberty or Give Me Death"* speech (see www.history.org/ almanac/life/politics/giveme.cfm

34. Emmanuel Kant. *Kant's Political Writings* (New York: Cambridge Univ. Press, 1970), pp.41-53.

35. Arthur Schopenhauer. *The World as Will and Representation*, Vol 1. (Mineola, NY: Dover Publications Inc., 1969), p.324.

36. *Leo Tolstoy. War and Peace, Second Epilogue. Publication of Pennsylvania State Univ. Electronic Classics Series, Jim Manis, Ed. (Hazelton, PA: Penn.State Univ, 2000), pp. 64-109.*

37. *Montgomery. op.cit., pp.164-165.*

38. *David Hume. "An Enquiry Concerning Human Understanding," Sect. VIII, Part 1. L.A. Selby-Bigge edition (Oxford at the Clarendon Press, 1972), p.84.*

39. Nietzsche, *On the Advantage and Disadvantage of History for Life*, 1874. transl. by Peter Preuss.(Indianapolis: Hackett Publishing Co., 1980), p.17.

40. Byle. op.cit., pp.290-291.

41. R.G. Collingwood. *The Idea of History*. (New York: Oxford Univ. Press edition, reprint from 1936, 1994), missing information

42. Pitirim A. Sorokin. *Social & Cultural Dynamics*. Reprint of the 1957 ed. (Transaction Publishers, 1985), p.683.

43. Byl. op.cit.,p.288.

Chap 5

44. Stanford. op.cit.,p.153

45. Ibid., pp.153-154.

46. Ibid., pp.77,80.

Chap 6

47. Clyde P. Greer, Jr. "Reflecting Honestly on History," in *Think Biblically!* John MacArthur, ed., op. cit., pp. 261-262.

Chap 7

48. Charles Colson and Nancy Pearcey. *How Now Shall We Live?* (Wheaton, Illinois: Tyndale House Publishers, Inc, 1999), p.228.

49. John Warwick Montgomery. *Tractatus Logico-Theologicus.* (Bonn: Verlag für Kultur und Wissenschaft, 2002), p.13.

Chap 9

50. Francis Schaeffer. "The God Who is There," in *Trilogy* (Wheaton, IL: Crossway Books, 1990), p. 113

Chap 10

51. Walter C. Kaiser Jr. *The Promise Plan of God: A Biblical Theology of the Old and new Testaments.* (Grand Rapids, MI: Zondervan, 2008), pp. 31, 283.

52. Pinchas Lapid. *Israelis, Jews and Jesus.* Garden City, NJ: Doubleday and Co, 1979, p. 2.

53. Walter C. Kaiser, Jr. *The Promise-Plan of God, op. cit.,p. 13.*

54. Hal Lindsey. *The Everlasting Hatred: The Roots of Jihad.* (Washington D.C.: WND Books, 2011), pp. 22-23.

55. Kaiser, op. cit., pp. 366-367

56. Daniel Gruber. *The Church and the Jews: The Biblical Relationship.* (Springfield, MO: General Council of the Assemblies of God, Intercultural Ministries, 1991), p. 65.

57. Ibid. p. 66

58. Don Samdahl. http://doctrine.org/the-olive-tree/. 2011 (updated April 16, 2012).

Chap 11

59. W.E. McCumber. *Was It Not I? And Other Questions God Asks* (Kansas City, MO: Beacon Hill Press, 1994), p.89.

60. A.W. Tozer. *The Knowledge of the Holy* (New York: Harper Collins, 1978), p.3.

61. D.L. Moody. *On the Ten Commandments.* (Chicago: Moody Publishers, 1896), p.16.

62. John MacArthur. *Commentary on First Corinthians.* (Chicago: Moody Publishers, 1984), pp. 232–233.

63. Daniel Henderson. "*The Subtle Seduction of Modern-Day Idolatry.*" (www.strategicrenewal.com).

64. Walter C. Kaiser, Jr. *Revive Us Again. (Nashville: Broadman & Holman Publishers, 1999), p. 8.*

65. Leclerc, Diane. *Discovering Christian Holiness: The Heart of Weleyan-Holiness Theology.* (Kansas City, MO: Beacon Hill Press, 2010), p. 61.

Chap 12

66. James W. Sire. *The Universe Next Door*, 5th ed. (Downers Grove, IL: Intervarsity Press, 2009), p. 85.

67. Nancy Pearcey. *Total Truth: Liberating Christianity from Its Cultural Captivity* (Wheaton, IL: Crossway Books, 2004), p. 35.

68. Ibid., p. 37.

69. Ibid., p. 40.

70. Ibid., p. 44.

71. Ibid., pp. 58-62.

72. Ibid., p. 90.

73. Ibid., p. 95.

Chap 13

74. Roger E. Olson. Counterfeit Christianity. (Nashville: Abingdon Press, 2015), p.5.

Chap 14

75. *Letter to Diognetus.* (transl. Paul Pavao). http://www.christian-history.org/letter-to-diognetus.html

76. James W. Sire. *The Universe Next Door, 5th Ed.* (Donners Grove, IL: Intervarsity Press, 2009), pp.283-284.

77. Norman Geisler and Peter Bocchino. *Unshakable Foundations: Contemporary Answers to Crucial Questions about the Christian Faith* (Bloomington, MN: Bethany House Publishers, 2001), pp.58-60.

APPENDIX A
DISCUSSION QUESTIONS FOR PART 1

- Each of the tenants outlined in Chapter 1 (pp.5-6) by John Byl can be compared to our prevailing culture. We must ask what in popular behavior and belief contradicts the Christian worldview.

- Taking each line, compare the Christian worldview as described by Byl with competing worldviews, with the view of many of your friends and family, with the current view as taught in American educational systems

- In what sense is ones worldview a "matter of life and death?"

- How can a consistent Christian worldview influence our culture?

- Use of the phrase "politically correct," is usually derisive; it suggests an absence of moral values and integrity of evaluation. What is the opposite of politically correct? What word or phrase comes to mind? Does that phrase reflect your Christian worldview?

APPENDIX B
A PARTIAL GLOSSARY (FOR CLARITY)

Agnosticism - nothing is known or can be known of the existence or nature of God or of anything beyond material phenomena; claiming neither faith nor disbelief in God.

Atheism - disbelief or lack of belief in the existence of God or gods.

Cosmology – the study of the physical universe considered as a totality of phenomena in time and space; a grand design, a system in which all of existence can be explained successfully

Deism – the belief in the existence of god by reason as indicated by what has been created; but such belief is not by revelation (as in theism); that god after setting up natural laws no longer is engaged in the affairs of men.

Deductive Reasoning - a logical process in which a conclusion is based on the concordance of multiple premises that are generally assumed to be true. Deductive reasoning is sometimes referred to as top-down logic.

Design and Purpose – the belief that there is a reason for all that happens in the larger scope of things and that there is a designer who ultimately is in control. Furthermore, it is the belief that the designer is not capricious or arbitrary in his creation, but that all things will be made clear in the long run.

Empirical – the gathering of evidence that is (or has been) seen, touched, heard, etc.; that which is derived from experience or experiment

Eschatology – the part of theology concerned with death, judgment and final destiny of the soul and of humankind and with those events leading to the culmination of all things

Epistemology – the examination of how we can know something is true, exists or is real rather than imagined. It is to consider the nature of knowledge, its foundations, its presuppositions, and its extent and validity.

Exegesis – the careful, systematic study of the Scripture to discover the original, intended meaning.

Finite Godism - God exists but is limited and finite.

General Revelation – the understanding that God's existence has been made clear by what has been created and that God has revealed Himself to all persons at all times and in all places by which humans come to know that God is and what He is like.

Hermeneutics – concerned with the nature of the interpretive process, including exegesis. In the narrower sense it is seeking the contemporary relevance of ancient texts. It is the final step in bringing God's Word to man.

Historical Apologetics – defending the faith according to historical evidence as the basis for demonstrating the truth of Christianity.

Historicism – a theory that history is determined by immutable laws and not by human agency; the search for laws of historical progression that would explain and predict

Historiography – the analytic philosophy of history, focusing on techniques such as the scientific method, probability theory or textual criticism; the rules for investigation

Inductive Reasoning - a logical process in which multiple premises, all believed true or found true most of the time, are combined to obtain a specific conclusion. Inductive reasoning is often used in applications that involve prediction, forecasting, or behavior. It is sometimes referred to as bottom-up logic.

Irony – the use of words or ideas to express something different from and often opposite to their literal meaning; incongruity between what might be expected and what actually occurs

Logical Positivism – a movement in Western philosophy, developed by members of the Vienna and Berlin Circles, that considers the only meaningful philosophical problems to be those that can be solved by logical analysis as in the empirical sciences.

Logos – the eternal Word of God

Metahistory – the speculative philosophy of history, looking for an overarching narrative that gives order and meaning to the historical record, esp. in the large scale philosophies of history such as Hegel, Marx or Spencer

Metaphor – a figure of speech in which a word or phrase that designates one thing is applied to another in an implicit comparison.

Metonymy – a figure of speech in which one word or phrase is substituted for another with which it is closely associated, e.g. Washington for U.S. government

Modernism – a philosophical movement in Western society in the late 19th and early 20th centuries which rejected the traditions of the arts and sciences as ill-fitted to a modern industrialized society.

Monotheism – the belief that there is only one God.

Natural Theology – the attempt to either prove God's existence, define God's attributes, or derive correct doctrine based soley on human reason and observation of the natural world.

Naturalism – Nature is the "whole show." There is no supernatural realm or intervention in the world. The term may be applied to all views that are not theistic.

Necessary Cause – in order for an event to have happened, this one thing must first have happened (though it may not be sufficient in and of itself)

Nihilism - the rejection of all religious and moral principles, often in the belief that life is meaningless.

Nomological – The study and discovery of general physical and logical laws.

Ontological – pertaining to the nature of existence

Pantheism – the view that God is everything and everyone and that everyone and everything is God.

Panentheism - considers God and the world to be inter-related with the world being in God and God being in the world. It offers an increasingly popular alternative to both traditional theism and pantheism.

Polytheism - the belief in or worship of more than one god.

Postmodernism – Following the industrial revolution and enlightenment of the 19th Century came 20th Century skepticism, existentialism, nihilism, logical positivism, deconstruction ism and relativism. Philosophers, artists and thinkers began to speak of art as "for its own sake," intentions were unknowable and it became more difficult to see purpose in our existence.

Presupposition – a tenant in one's worldview. A presupposition is foundational. It requires no further proof and is a settled matter for the person holding it. It rises above presumption in that it is accepted on strong authority.

"Proof-texting" – Having a man-made idea (as one thinks things should be) and then finding a scripture to back it up, rather than developing ones ideas from the Word of God.

Relativism – the denial of absolute truth. Things may appear to be true but from another vantage point may not. Of course if there is no absolute truth, no one is really ever wrong. One person's truth is just as good as the next person's.

Revelation – God reveals Himself to us through what He has created (general), through history (progressive) and through intervention in our own lives (special).

Selective Sampling – Human beings often see what they want to see and ignore what does not fit their paradigms. The truth can be avoided by choosing to see only what supports one's view and ignoring that which contradicts it. Such a person is said to be biased or prejudiced.

Skepticism – a doctrine which finds true knowledge uncertain.

Special Revelation – the discovery of God and of spiritual matters through means other than man's reason, such as the testimony of Scripture, miracles or supernatural means.

Speculative – that which is advanced by reason alone (in contrast to empirical)

Sufficient Cause – for causal relationship this cause or set of causes taken together are all necessary for the event to have happened

Synecdoche – a figure of speech in which a part is used for the whole, e.g. the law for police officer or steel for a sword

Teleology – the study of design or purpose in natural phenomena; purposeful development toward a final end

Tests of coherence, experience and livability – These should be applied in order to validate any worldview according to author   John Byl.

Theism – belief in the existence of a god or gods, especially belief in one god as creator of the universe, intervening in it and sustaining a personal relation to his creatures.

Transcendent God – over all in authority, power and understanding. God transcends our   abilities and our knowledge in every way. He is all-powerful, all-knowing and eternal.

Tropology – the study of the use and effect of tropes, metaphors or archetypes in literary expression

Worldview – how one views or interprets reality. It is the framework by which one makes sense of the data of life. A worldview makes a world of difference in one's view of God, origins, evil, human nature, values and destiny.

APPENDIX C
INDEX OF AUTHORS AND PERSONS
(other than Biblical, mentioned or quoted)

APPENDIX D
WORLDVIEW ANALOGIES & QUESTIONS FOR DISCUSSION

Metaphors:
1) History as DRAMA
2) History as REPETITION
3) History as EVOLUTION
4) History as STRUGGLE
5) History as SCIENCE
6) History as PROPOGANDA
7) History as RANDOM OCCURRENCE
8) History as GOD'S PROVIDENCE

Using the eight worldview analogies, discuss the following:

1. How does one's view of history effect his life and faith?
   A. The way he talks about the major issues of life?
   B. The way he makes choices?
   C. The way he thinks about death?

2. How does one's view of history effect his defense of the faith?
   A. Is the biblical presentation of Christ consistent with his worldview?
   B. How important is history in a balanced argument for the faith?
   C. How should one best approach a person in presenting the Gospel?

ABOUT THE AUTHOR

Paul M. Ethington was born in 1946 in Illinois to a bi-vocational pastor/ teacher/ musician, Oakley Ethington. Raised in the Midwest, educated in California and Alaska, in and around the Church of the Nazarene, he developed a deep love for the Scriptures. For the last five decades he has conducted Bible Studies in small groups almost continuously. Squarely in the middle of orthodox Christianity he may be described as Wesleyan and an evangelical. He obtained his B.S. in philosophy and M.S. in music from Cal State Fullerton. Although his vocation has been electrician, he is an avid reader whose hobby is biblical theology and passion is teaching. His habit of preparing his own curriculum and materials has led to many book manuscripts. Only recently has he attempted to publish. His penchant for taking complex material and organizing it for ease of understanding makes him very readable. He challenges his students to know Jesus more deeply as they go through life. He is not afraid to ask hard questions and to discuss Bible difficulties. His intention is to be more clear than clever and his style is expositional. He admits that he does not know everything, and that drives him to be an avid student who reads others' work. Yet, he is convinced that the Word of God is accessible to all and that remains his primary reference and focus; what do the Scriptures say? Mr. Ethington says that experience is instructive, though skewed. Tradition is important, though selective. Logic and conceptual analysis are helpful, though subject to artful manipulation. Only the Scriptures by the teaching of the Holy Spirit are trustworthy. With thorough exegesis Paul Ethington is determined to communicate this teaching to hungry hearts by the help of the Holy Spirit. He lives in Northern Idaho now with his wife Maria. Having spent most of their lives in SoCal and three years in Alaska, they are enjoying the four seasons. He has two grown children, Marisol and David. All of them are solid Christians active in their local settings. Still, there is a larger family who Mr. Ethington enjoys wherever he goes who love the Lord and look forward to His coming. His love for music allowed him to lead singing for forty years in the Church of the Nazarene. His love for people causes him to reach outside the walls of the church with frequent visits to missions where he plays the piano, sings and gives his testimony for the encouragement of all who seek Jesus.

Made in the USA
Columbia, SC
18 February 2021

33207592R00106